ORTHO'S All About

Lawns

Meredith® Books
Des Moines, Iowa

Ortho All About Lawns
Editor: Michael McKinley
Contributing Editor: Veronica Lorson Fowler
Contributing Technical Editor: Ashton Ritchie
Photo Researcher: Harijs Priekulis
Copy Chief: Terri Fredrickson
Publishing Operations Manager: Karen Schirm
Edit and Design Production Coordinator: Mary Lee Gavin
Editorial and Design Assistants: Kathleen Stevens,
    Kairee Windsor
Marketing Product Managers: Aparna Pande, Isaac Petersen,
    Gina Rickert, Stephen Rogers, Brent Wiersma,
    Tyler Woods
Book Production Managers: Pam Kvitne,
    Marjorie J. Schenkelberg, Rick von Holdt, Mark Weaver
Contributing Copy Editor: Barbara Feller-Roth,
Technical Proofreader: Patrick Smythe-Eagle
Contributing Proofreaders: Elise J. Marton, Margaret Smith
Contributing Map Illustrator: Jana Fothergill
Indexer: Ellen Davenport

**Additional Editorial Contributions from
    Roundtable Press, Inc.**
Directors: Marsha Melnick, Julie Merberg
Designer: Annemarie Redmond
Illustrator: Elayne Sears

Meredith® Books
Executive Director, Editorial: Gregory H. Kayko
Executive Director, Design: Matt Strelecki
Executive Editor/Group Manager: Benjamin W. Allen
Senior Associate Design Director: Tom Wegner
Publisher and Editor in Chief: James D. Blume

Editorial Director: Linda Raglan Cunningham
Executive Director, Marketing: Jeffrey B. Myers
Executive Director, New Business Development:
    Todd M. Davis
Executive Director, Sales: Ken Zagor
Director, Operations: George A. Susral
Director, Production: Douglas M. Johnston
Business Director: Jim Leonard

Vice President and General Manager: Douglas J. Guendel

Meredith Publishing Group
President: Jack Griffin
Senior Vice President: Bob Mate

Meredith Corporation
Chairman and Chief Executive Officer: William T. Kerr
President and Chief Operating Officer: Stephen M. Lacy

In Memoriam: E.T. Meredith III (1933–2003)

Note to the Readers: Due to differing conditions, tools, and individual skills, Meredith Corporation assumes no responsibility for any damages, injuries suffered, or losses incurred as a result of following the information published in this book. Before beginning any project, review the instructions carefully, and if any doubts or questions remain, consult local experts or authorities. Because codes and regulations vary greatly, you always should check with authorities to ensure that your project complies with all applicable local codes and regulations. Always read and observe all of the safety precautions provided by manufacturers of any tools, equipment, or supplies, and follow all accepted safety procedures.

Thanks to: Janet Anderson, Staci Bailey, Diane Witosky

Photographers
(Photographers credited may retain copyright ©
    to the listed photographs.)
L = Left, R = Right, C = Center, B = Bottom, T = Top

William D. Adams: 12, 17R, 21, 30, 34, 39, 41, 49B, 71R, 80R,
    89TR, 112TR
Crandall & Crandall: 31, 32, 35
Gary Elfert: 94BL, 97T, 103B
Derek Fell: 10L, 16T, 17L, 22, 26, 37B, 48T, 48BL, 70BL
Roger Foley: 8, 33, 60T, 66, 67, 75, 79
John Glover: 1, 7T, 9T, 10R, 13, 63B, 80L, 118B
Larry Kassell: 19
Dwight Kuhn: 18T
Charles Mann: 7B, 28, 29, 37T, 43
J. Paul Moore: 24, 48BR
Philip Nixon: 110T, 112B, 113T, 114C, 115C,
Jerry Pavia: 3T, 5, 11T, 11B, 36, 70TL
Wayne Philips: 27
Larry Sagers: 18B, 71L, 82B, 89BR
Bill Scheffler: 101T
Albert Squillace: 6B, 14, 44, 47C, 63T, 70TR
Michael Thompson: 25, 47B, 89TL,
Michelle Tripplestone: 9B, 16B, 38, 47T, 54L, 70BR, 96B,
    101C, 102C
Mark Turner: 6T, 42, 63C, 94TL, 98T
Tom Voigt: 89BR
Jessie Walker: 4, 40

All of us at Meredith® Books are dedicated to providing you with the information and ideas you need to enhance your home and garden. We welcome your comments and suggestions about this book. Write to us at:
    Meredith Corporation
    Meredith Gardening Books
    1716 Locust St.
    Des Moines, IA 50309–3023

If you would like to purchase any of our gardening, home improvement, cooking, crafts, or home decorating and design books, check wherever quality books are sold. Or visit us at: meredithbooks.com

If you would like more information on other Ortho products, call 800/225-2883 or visit us at: www.ortho.com

PLAN AHEAD FOR A
Great Lawn

Americans love their lawns. From Maine to California, nothing defines the look of our towns and suburbs like lawns. Large or small, lawns are an essential part of American life. We ask a lot from our lawns. We demand that they look good while we use them hard for entertaining, sports, relaxing, and playing. This use—and often abuse—is a challenge for the turfgrasses in the lawn. Yet no other plant is as well-suited to this task. Turfgrasses are the only kind of groundcover that can tolerate continual foot traffic and still look good.

Our lawns do more for us than we may realize. Lawns cushion our steps and our children's falls, buffer noise, and cool the air. Lawns prevent erosion and absorb pollutants. They trap dust and dirt. They soak up rainfall and filter contaminants from water. They release oxygen into the atmosphere. They take constant abuse and keep coming back for more.

The classic emerald sward that has been the epitome of the great American lawn takes work and commitment. If you want that ideal lawn, the effort is worth it. But research and real-world experience have shown that turf gets by with less input than once thought possible. Some new grass varieties require much less overall maintenance than others. Decide how much work you want to put into your lawn and what you want it to look like, then plan accordingly.

The first step toward having a lawn you love is to assess what you need from a lawn. Writing your thoughts and ideas down on paper makes the planning process easier and less confusing. After you go through the assessment process that follows, you can use your conclusions as the basis for redesigning and improving your lawn or creating a new lawn from scratch.

Assessing your lawn needs

Your lawn should suit your lifestyle and work for you. What you want from your lawn, in a physical sense and a visual one, plays a major role in what kind of lawn you

A smooth expanse of luxurious lawn sets off your home beautifully, and its benefits continue. Your lawn improves the health and well-being of everyone around it.

Consider how you'll use each area of your lawn before you choose a grass variety. Remember that if you choose an appropriate grass, one of its advantages will be a soft landing.

HOW DO YOU USE YOUR LAWN?

What features exist in your lawn and how do you use the yard?

- ■ Children's swing set/play area
- ■ Sports and other recreational activities
- ■ Swimming pool
- ■ Outdoor dining/entertaining
- ■ Sitting, relaxing, reading
- ■ Sunbathing
- ■ Strolling
- ■ Gardening
  - □ Flower gardens
  - □ Vegetable and herb gardens
  - □ Shrub borders
  - □ Trees
- ■ Containing and/or exercising pets
- ■ Feeding/sheltering/observing birds and other wildlife
- ■ Parking for cars

should have: how big, what shape, what kind of turf. Your climate and unique site make up the rest of the equation.

To assess what you need in a lawn, begin by making a list of ways your family uses the lawn, including things you might like to do but can't now because the lawn will not accommodate them. Use the checklist "How Do You Use Your Lawn?" (above right) as a place to start, and make your own list of things you would like to do on your lawn. The answers will begin to guide your planning. For instance, if your children want a play area or grownups would like a game of touch football or croquet, you need tough turf that can take a lot of foot traffic. If you like to sit quietly outdoors to enjoy a book or take a break with a cool drink, you need quiet, shady places with shade-tolerant grass. If your yard is friendly to wildlife and you enjoy feeding the birds and chipmunks, you can consider a more natural kind of lawn, with some areas of taller

grass. If you have garden beds and borders, the lawn can be shaped to integrate gardens and walkways so the landscape works together as a whole. If you need additional

parking, you might need to shrink the lawn to provide more space for cars. You might even choose more than one type of lawn to suit all of your needs.

WHAT OUR LAWNS DO FOR US

Our lawns are our private green space. They give us places to play and relax; they showcase our gardens and frame our homes. But lawns do a lot more. Here are some things you might not know our lawns do for us.

CLEAN THE AIR: About 12 million tons of dust and dirt are trapped by turfgrasses every year.

CUSHION US: In a test of turfgrass cushioning effects, a dozen eggs were dropped from a height of 11 feet; none broke on a dense lawn.

KEEP US DRY: Healthy lawns absorb lots of water, keeping our yards from becoming muddy after a rainfall.

KEEP OUR SPIRITS UP: Studies at hospitals show that people heal more quickly when they see a patch of green grass.

PREVENT EROSION: Because grass plants are 90% roots, they are efficient at preventing erosion.

FILTER WATER: Lawns filter runoff pollutants that could otherwise enter underground aquifers.

RAISE REAL ESTATE VALUE: A healthy lawn and landscape can add about 15% to the value of a home.

HELP US BREATHE: Even a small lawn (50 square feet) regularly releases enough oxygen for a family of four and absorbs carbon dioxide, ozone, and hydrogen fluoride.

COOL THE AIR: Just eight average-size lawns on a single city block will provide the same cooling effect as a 70-ton air-conditioner.

EASE ALLERGIES: Grasses filter and absorb pollen as well as dust, trapping allergens that irritate many people.

MINIMIZE FIRE DAMAGE: Lawns can slow the spread of a fire.

FEED OUR FEATHERED FRIENDS: A healthy lawn provides insects, worms, and other food for birds.

Lawns in Your Landscape

A well-designed lawn connects different areas of your landscape, integrating flower beds and borders into a harmonious whole.

Simple and unassuming, grass is the perfect backdrop for flamboyant flowers. Here, it complements the color of spring-blooming peonies.

We don't think about it much, but a lawn is a major element in the design of a home landscape. A lawn connects the house to the other parts of the property: the sidewalk or street, the garage, the driveway, garden beds and borders, sheds and other outbuildings. The lawn flows around all these pieces and unites them into a whole.

The lawn is the green ground upon which the garden's colors show off—it sets the stage for the garden's show. Its horizontal plane contrasts with the vertical lines of trees and trellises. An expanse of lawn makes a property feel more open and spacious. A swath of green has psychological benefits too. Green is the most restful color to look at because the lens of our eye does not have to refocus in order to perceive it. A green lawn offers visual relief from even the most bright color flowers, softening what might otherwise be a discordant clash of hues.

Given the many roles the lawn plays in the landscape,

PRACTICAL CONSIDERATIONS

Whether you're putting in a totally new lawn or assessing an existing one, it's to your advantage to pay attention to factors that affect the way your lawn will grow. Planning around these conditions is much easier than trying to overcome them.

- Will the lawn get full sun? And will that situation change in the near future due to growth of trees, new outbuildings, and so forth? Different grasses thrive in either sun or shade; choose one that is appropriate.
- If your lawn must contend with poor drainage, wind, and heat stress, choose grass varieties that can do so.
- How much maintenance can you handle? You can choose a regime that allows low, medium, or high maintenance.
- How good do you need the lawn to look? Can you limit areas that need to be perfect? Consider dividing your site into sections, with some receiving more care than others.
- What's your budget? Think about what you can spend now and what your lawn will cost in the coming years. If you prefer not to pay for upkeep, it's better to install a low-maintenance lawn.

DESIGN CHOICES

Color and texture are aesthetic considerations when choosing a grass. Grasses come in many colors: blue-greens, bright greens, gray-greens, even powder blues. Textures range from smooth and silky to spiky. You might want to choose a grass that greens up early to highlight your spring bulbs or one that stays green longer to provide a backdrop to the fall foliage of your sugar maples.

In a complex garden such as this one, a smooth, horizontal plane of grass allows each element to shine. Instead of feeling busy and cluttered, the garden seems relaxed and comforting.

it should be a part of the overall design of your property, not just an afterthought that fills in the space between the other elements. For the lawn to work properly and pull the landscape together, it has to be the right size and shape. This takes planning. If you are designing a new lawn or redesigning an existing one, after you have assessed what you need the lawn to do in a practical way, think about it from a designer's point of view, considering elements such as subtle differences in grass color and texture.

Look at your property from outside it, by standing in the street or down the block, to see how it looks to the rest of the neighborhood. Over a period of several weeks or even months, think about the different roles you'd like the lawn to play in your landscape. Consider using several types of lawn instead of just one and imagine how the different sections could be integrated.

This natural landscape incorporates several elements melded together with lawn. The gray-green color and rough texture of the blue gramagrass lawn is a perfect foil for the earth-tone house and free-form shrubs.

What's Your Style?

Though a lawn might be the simplest, most straightforward element in the landscape, it does have style. You can find the right style for your lawn by looking at the style of your house and grounds.

If your house is formal, your lawn should be too. Formal landscapes are designed more or less in a grid pattern. The lawn is rectangular or square, with neat, straight edges. Informal landscapes employ more curved lines. Beds and borders are often designed in rounded shapes, and the lawn follows their graceful contours. (See page 10 for more about shaped lawns.)

(See page 10 for more about shaped lawns.)

DESIGN ISSUES

Look at what your lawn is like now and assess its current condition. Here are some questions to ask. Write down your answers to use as you continue the design process.

- How big is the lawn? How is it shaped?
- Is the lawn too big? Do you have too much green and too little color in your landscape?
- Is the lawn too small?
- Does the shape of the lawn allow you to move easily through the landscape? Does the lawn flow smoothly around garden beds and borders? Does it complement your house? Would a different shape work better?
- Is the lawn easy to mow, or does it have too many sharp corners? Is it easy to get the lawn mower to all parts of the yard? Are there hard-to-mow slopes? Do you have trouble mowing around tree trunks? Do you have to duck under branches as you mow?
- Does the lawn have a neat edge where it meets garden beds and walkways? Is it difficult to edge the lawn?

This cottage garden includes swaying foxglove, artemisia, and roses, arranged casually. The lawn reflects the informal style of the garden. It isn't perfectly manicured and doesn't need to be.

A formal garden, with structured plants, a symmetrical arrangement, and elaborate pathways is well served by a carefully tended lawn that is kept in perfect condition.

terrain and microclimates of your yard. For example, it is difficult to establish a good lawn on a steep slope. The grass seed tends to wash away, and slopes are dangerous to mow as well as difficult to water adequately. Planting ground covers rather than turfgrass may be the most appropriate solution for a slope.

Think about future irrigation needs when planning your lawn. If you will be watering with a sprinkler, avoid creating nooks and crannies that will require extra fussing with the sprinkler to avoid dry spots in the lawn.

A lawn in a woodland setting is casual, meandering around trees and shrubs. Consider regional influences: an adobe house in the Southwest is beautifully complemented by rough native grasses, whereas an urban rooftop could be enhanced by a tiny patch of velvety bentgrass. A soft, cool lawn of Kentucky bluegrass would work well in a sunbathing area around a pool and one of shade-tolerant fescue in a meditation garden.

Grasses can also be chosen for their stylistic elements: rough, smooth, dense, and coarse. See the Gallery of Grasses on pages 20–37.

Plan for easy care

Think about maintenance when you are designing or redesigning a lawn. There are several ways to reduce future maintenance while creating a pleasing design. For example, if trees are in lawn areas,

group them together in large beds with shrubs and ground covers. At the very least, create a wide mulched area around each tree to avoid nicking bark with the mower as well as to make mowing easier. These mulched areas also help the tree become established faster because they eliminate competition from grass roots.

In areas that will be heavily trafficked, use paving or other hardscaping from the start. Then there'll be no need to repair or replace the "cow paths" that develop. Use a wear-tolerant turfgrass in play areas or consider mulching the entire area instead of planting grass.

To simplify mowing, avoid creating awkward corners among the plantings. Also, make sure every patch of lawn is accessible with the mower. Trying to get the mower up several stairs or through a narrow passage will make mowing a much less desirable chore.

Be sure to consider the

A woodland setting calls for a simple lawn. The site is usually larger than a backyard, so a low-maintenance lawn is practical as well as aesthetically pleasing.

Edgings, Paths, and Shapes

A lawn can be whatever shape works best to connect garden beds, trees, paths, and other elements in the yard. In an informal landscape, the lawn flows in sinuous curves around garden beds and groupings of trees. As your eyes follow its flowing lines, the lawn visually draws you farther into the landscape. In a formal landscape, rectangular or square patches of lawn are arranged symmetrically around geometric garden beds. In a small front yard, accent and emphasize the crisp shape of a square lawn with rectangular garden borders around the perimeter and a fence along the street side.

A lawn can be designed in practically any shape you need. But avoid carving up the lawn into little patches. Its beauty lies in sweeping expanse. Also, avoid cutting the edges of the lawn into little scallops or notches; gently flowing curves or straight lines look more graceful and are easier to mow and edge.

Use trees, shrubs, and other features to punctuate the horizontal plane of the lawn and add interest to the scene. Avoid putting too many features in the lawn. Individual trees planted here and there, along with many garden beds and statuary or ornaments, dilute the effect of a smooth green expanse of lawn and are hard to mow around.

Edgings

The shape of a lawn is defined by its edges. A well-defined edge where the lawn meets garden beds and paths gives the landscape a neat, clean look. In a formal landscape, crisp edging contributes to the precision of the overall design.

Edging also serves the practical function of keeping the lawn from spreading beyond its boundaries. Lawn grasses like to travel, and some, such as Bermudagrass, spread aggressively. If the lawn grows right up to the garden, the grass will migrate among the flowers. Edging will keep the lawn where it belongs. Edging also defines where the flower bed begins and the lawn stops.

You can edge a lawn in a number of ways. The simplest is to use a spade or an edging tool to leave a narrow strip of bare soil between the lawn and the garden or path. For a permanent solution, you can install an edging of cobblestone, bricks standing on end, concrete paving stones, or metal or plastic edging strips along the boundary between lawn and garden or walkway.

For ease of maintenance, install a mowing strip next to the edging. A mowing strip is a border of stones, bricks, or concrete pavers set into the ground with their surface flush with the ground. When you mow the grass, two wheels of the mower travel over the mowing strip, allowing you to mow right to the edge of the lawn. You won't have to bother with

A curvy border of gravel provides an edge between lawn and flower beds. This clear-cut definition makes mowing and weeding easier.

Low boxwood shrubs enclose this garden that draws together the lawn and surrounding trees. Just a few spring alliums and a rhododendron provide plenty of color.

TIPS ON TECHNIQUES

Here are two simple but effective procedures for permanent improvements to your lawn.

SETTING FLAGSTONES: Trace the shape of the stone and dig out the soil 6 inches deeper than the stone. Fill the hole with 5 inches of crushed stone or gravel and 2 inches of sand. Then position the flagstone. The sand will fill in the holes between the gravel or crushed stone, and foot traffic will secure the flagstone.

CREATING AN EDGING: Rent a bedding edger to make fast work of edging with steel, plastic, or stone. After using the bedding edger, it's almost child's play to install a plastic edging between lawn and flower bed. Fill in with soil and top with about 2 inches of mulch.

Installing a stone pathway is easy. It keeps traffic off the grass and provides an interesting design element.

time-consuming hand-trimming, and you won't risk damaging garden plants when you cut the grass.

Paths

Paths are an essential part of any yard. They enable you to get from one place to another easily, and they save wear and tear on the lawn. If you don't have paths on well-traveled routes, the grass will be worn away.

Where to put paths in your yard is often obvious. You know you have to get to the door, to the garage, and to the swimming pool, for example. But you may also be taking shortcuts across the lawn or using routes you aren't consciously aware of. If you see trails across the lawn where the grass is wearing thin, you probably need to put paths there.

If you want to create a walkway that is unobtrusive,

you can simply set stepping-stones into the lawn. Stepping-stones can be flagstone, bricks laid together in squares, wood disks, or concrete rounds. Stepping-stones set in a lawn create a lovely effect.

Main paths that lead to important destinations such as the front door need to be clearly defined to show visitors where to walk. Make these paths of brick, flagstone, poured concrete, pavers, gravel, or other durable material.

Sometimes grass can be a path too. Grass makes a soft, attractive surface for paths that don't carry heavy traffic. One likely place for a grass path is between garden beds. If you want to use lawn to surface a path, make sure the path is wide enough to mow easily. Three feet is about the minimum width. Be sure to keep the path neatly edged.

Carefully shaped and rounded, this lawn enhances the entrance to a contemporary home.

Contours for Easy Care

If your lawn is on well-drained ground that is reasonably level, consider yourself lucky. Good drainage is critical for a healthy lawn. Ideally, the ground should slope gently away from the house out toward the edges of the lawn. That will allow water to drain away instead of collecting in your basement.

Water naturally flows downhill, seeking the lowest spot. If water collects in low places on the lawn, it will eventually cause grass roots to rot. The water fills the spaces between soil particles and drives out the air, which is essential for healthy roots. The grass suffocates. Fixing a poor grade can improve drainage for the lawn.

Yes, you can have a rolling lawn, even on a small site. Contouring your site adds dimension to everything that's planted on it; it pulls your eye and your interest along with it.

If your yard has a lot of humps and dips, consider regrading to improve the drainage. The lawn doesn't have to be perfectly level, especially in an informally designed landscape. In fact, a lawn that follows gently rolling terrain can be quite appealing. But deep hollows and big bumps all over the lawn make mowing difficult—the mower misses the low spots and scalps the high spots. A lumpy lawn is also hard to use for recreational activities.

You also may need to repair the grade if you have a large tree removed from your yard.

Another place to consider regrading is on a hillside. It's hard to mow a slope; in fact,

mowing a steep slope can be dangerous. You might be able to regrade a moderate-size hill that is too steep to mow. Another option is to create terraces to gain more usable space. Or you could plant the hill with ground covers and forgo the lawn there entirely.

Regrading can transform land that is essentially flat and uninteresting. Building a berm or a gentle slope can add interest to the property. A berm along a property line can give you more privacy too, especially with a row of shrubs or ornamental grasses planted along the top.

For major regrading jobs you'll need to hire a contractor with a tractor or

other equipment. You may be able to tackle small jobs yourself. To contour an area for a new lawn, start by removing the topsoil in wheelbarrow loads and piling it on a tarp in another area. Scrape off the tops of bumps remaining in the subsoil and fill in low spots. As you work, be mindful of the direction in which the water will drain; be sure you don't channel water toward the house. Tamp down the soil, then water well to settle it. Otherwise, it will settle later and you may end up with new bumps and dips. When you are satisfied with the contour, replace the topsoil in an even layer and rake it smooth.

Regrading an existing lawn is more difficult. To avoid ruining the lawn, do the grade work gradually, over a period of years if necessary. To fill in small, shallow low spots, spread a blend of good topsoil, such as Scotts® LawnSoil, or garden loam and peat moss ½ inch deep on top of the existing grass. Repeat the process twice a year, in spring and fall, until the holes are filled.

For larger depressions, remove the sod by slicing into it vertically to outline squares, then push a spade horizontally under the sod to sever the roots. Pull or roll back the sod and fill the hole with good topsoil or garden loam. Tamp down the soil, then replace the sod. Step on the sod or pull a heavy roller over it to give it good contact with the soil, then water it well.

WORKING WITH A PROFESSIONAL

Planting a new lawn is not difficult; most homeowners can do a good job. If your site requires major alteration, sometimes it's better to call someone who has more equipment, experience, and expertise. Unless you are particularly handy, the following lawn jobs are probably best done by professionals.

■ Installing drainage tile or ditches
■ Large-scale contouring, terracing, or regrading. Moving around a few wheelbarrows of dirt is easy, but if you have a large lawn and want to change its contours, earthmoving equipment will make it easier.
■ Installing pathways, decks, or complicated lighting systems
■ Installing very large lawns. Pros have access to hydroseeding equipment, which allows them to spread seed more quickly and evenly.

Once you decide to hire a professional landscape designer or landscape architect, do some homework to make sure you get the most for your money. (Architects are licensed; designers may or may not be, depending on what state they work in.) Rather than seeking professionals through advertisements in directories, talk to local nurseries, extension agents (see Resources, page 122), and Master Gardener programs for recommendations and suggestions. Most important, ask your neighbors. If you drive by a good-looking lawn, ask who put it in (most people like being told that their lawn is beautiful). When you choose a professional, ask for references and check them out.

A competent professional will want to know everything about your site and how you want to transform it. You should be able to provide that information in detail. Write down everything you can about your site and how it will be used (see How Do You Use Your Lawn? on page 5). Decide how much money you can spend, how much time you can devote to lawn care (or whether you can hire a

If a major project is planned, consider consulting a lawn-care professional. Do your homework before you meet.

lawn-care service), and whether you plan changes in the near or distant future. Allow time for consultation and planning; the winter is a good time to start. You should make a written agreement that includes the following:

■ How much the job and the professional services will cost.
■ How long it will take.
■ What future care will be required.
■ What state or local regulations must be taken into account.
■ What materials will be used, including plant materials and types of grasses. Be as specific as possible about what kind of grass seed or mix will be used and whether seed, sod, sprigs, or plugs will be used.
■ What techniques and equipment will be used and who will perform the work.
■ What kind of insurance the professional carries.

Once you have recommendations from your professional, check them out with local experts. Working with a pro will usually result in a spectacular lawn, but you can improve your chances of getting what you want by putting in a little work yourself as well.

THE RIGHT GRASS FOR A
Great Lawn

The right grass is the one that will thrive in your climate, require only the amount of work you're willing to provide, and complement your site.

Grasses are members of the family Poaceae, a group of 700 genera and 7,000 species, including bamboo, corn, and the well-adapted plants that make up our lawns.

Grass is a survivor, an ancient plant that evolved over millions of years in sun-filled prairies and meadows where large animals grazed on it. The densely formed grasses that survived in these ancient ecosystems were the ones with crowns that hugged the ground—out of the grazers' reach. The heritage and genetic makeup of these grasses have served them well. The turfgrasses in our lawns today are descendants of those early plants.

Although many of us spend plenty of time maintaining and enjoying our lawns—mowing them, fertilizing them, and just playing on them—few of us ever examine the plants themselves. If we did take a closer look, we would see their intricacy and variety.

All turfgrasses grow from a ground-hugging growth point, an area at the base of the plant called the *crown*. Today, except for the occasional rabbit, animals no longer graze on the grasses in our lawn. Our mowers clip them instead. As long as the crown is not damaged, the plant will survive.

Roots and shoots originate from the crown. Belowground, the fibrous root system, whose length can vary considerably from one species to another, absorbs nutrients and water from the soil and anchors the plant. Aboveground, stems and leaves take in light and carbon dioxide.

Extending upward from the crown, the *primary shoot* is the first to develop from a germinating seed. It—and every subsequent shoot—consists of leaves borne on short stems. A leaf consists of a *blade* and a *sheath*, the blade being the broad upper portion and the sheath the lower portion that encircles the stem. The sheath remains wrapped around the stem, whereas the blade unfurls and grows upward.

The sheath and blade meet at a point called the *collar*. Inside the collar is the *ligule,* a thin membranous band or ring of hairs, which ends in earlike lobes called *auricles*. The size, shape, and makeup of ligules and auricles provide valuable clues for identifying a grass.

Both the blades and sheaths originate from *nodes,* which are bulbous joints on the stems. There are several nodes on each stem (including spreading stems); the portions between them are called *internodes*. Several blades, sheaths, nodes, and internodes can exist on a primary shoot. Nodes and internodes don't develop until the grass plant starts to flower; then the internodes begin to elongate. Timely mowing reduces flowering, keeping internodes compact.

Tillers are secondary shoots that also grow from the crown. As they expand, they help make a lawn thick and full. All grasses exhibit some tiller growth, but the class known as bunchgrasses has especially heavy tiller activity. Because of these plentiful tillers arising from the crown, bunchgrasses, such as chewings, hard and tall fescues, and the ryegrasses, form thick clumps as they expand and fill a lawn.

Creeping grasses spread primarily by specialized stems—rhizomes and stolons—that extend horizontally from the crown of the parent plant.

Rhizomes are creeping stems that travel belowground, whereas *stolons* (or runners) travel aboveground. Some creeping grasses, such as

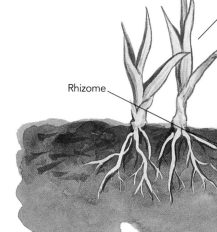

Rhizome

Kentucky bluegrass and red fescue, spread by rhizomes; some, such as centipedegrass and St. Augustinegrass, spread by stolons; another group, including both Bermudagrass and zoysiagrass, spreads by both rhizomes and stolons.

As they grow, stolons and rhizomes produce new plants at their nodes, each plant with its own set of roots. A *secondary shoot,* similar to the primary shoot of the parent plant, develops when a node on a rhizome or stolon roots and sprouts.

The turfgrass plant is unlike anything else growing in the landscape. Understanding its structure and growth is the first step in building a foundation for high-quality lawn care.

GRASS ANATOMY

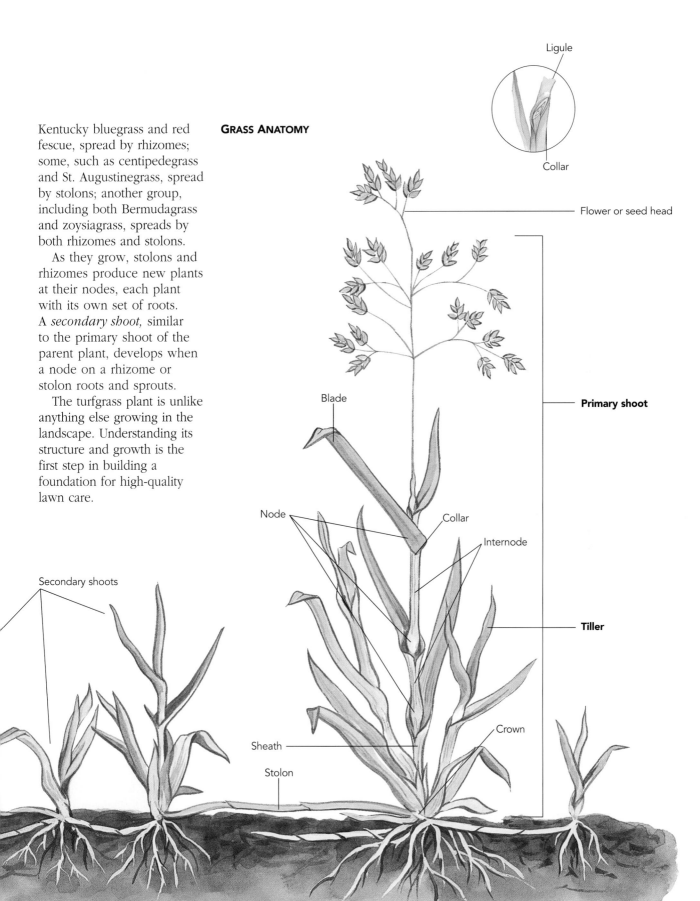

Ligule

Collar

Flower or seed head

Primary shoot

Blade

Node

Collar

Internode

Tiller

Secondary shoots

Sheath

Crown

Stolon

Classes of Grasses

The map on page 17 shows the five major climatic regions for turfgrass in the United States. It will help you further narrow your choice of grasses.

Cool-season grasses, such as the Kentucky bluegrass shown above, are at their best in the North, where summers are relatively cool and moist. They thrive—growing fast, thick, and green—during spring and again in autumn.

As summer turns to fall, cool-season grasses begin to brown and go dormant. Most cool-season grasses are cold hardy and will begin to grow again as soon as the snow melts.

Cool-humid

This is a diverse region that includes areas with mild, wet winters and warm, dry summers, and ones with frigid winters and hot summers. Rainfall totals 30 inches or more per year. All of the cool-season grasses grow well here, although where little rain falls in summer, they may go dormant for short periods unless watered. Zoysiagrass also grows in the southern portion of this region and along the Atlantic coast. It has a very short growing season here and is brown much of the year. Buffalograss grows in western areas of the region.

Cool-arid

Cold to mild, snowy to dry winters, and warm to hot, dry summers define this region. Rainfall totals less than 20 inches per year. Cool-season grasses, especially Kentucky bluegrass and fine fescue, grow here but must be irrigated to stay green. In warm parts, buffalograss does well without irrigation.

Warm-arid

Hot summer temperatures, mild winters, and little to no rain at any time of year are the norm here. As in the warm-humid region, warm-season grasses grow here, with bermudagrass the most common. Buffalograss can be grown in northern parts of the region. Because the soil is very alkaline and often saline, some of the minor grasses may be more appropriate for parts of this region.

Warm-humid

Winters are mild, rainfall is high, and summers are hot and humid. The area along the Gulf Coast is almost tropical, with rainfall totalling 60 inches or more per year. Warm-season grasses dominate

PRACTICAL CONSIDERATIONS

Warm-season grasses grow best when the weather is warm—in late spring through summer and into early fall. Cool-season grasses do best in the cool temperatures of spring and fall. Let this seasonality of growth guide you to the best times for major lawn maintenance projects.

Whenever tackling tasks that essentially "tear up" the grass, such as dethatching, aerating, or renovating the lawn, do them either early in the period of most active growth or just before growth starts. Scheduling these jobs early in the grass's season allows the turf to recover and fill in before the temperature changes for the worse for the grass.

The times to work on cool-season grasses are early spring, or late summer to early fall. Early to midsummer is best for warm-season grasses. When renovating cool-season lawns, be aware that competition from germinating weed seeds is lowest in late summer to early fall, so this may be the best time to schedule this task.

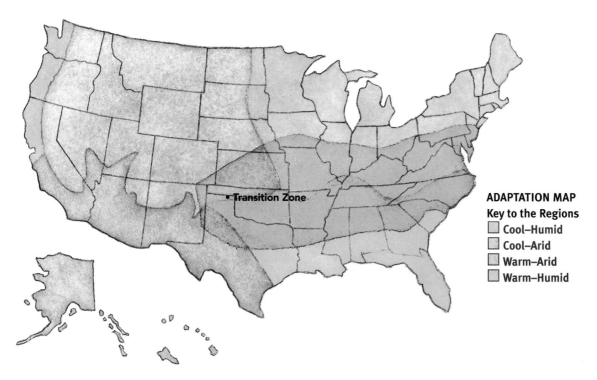

ADAPTATION MAP
Key to the Regions
☐ Cool–Humid
☐ Cool–Arid
☐ Warm–Arid
☐ Warm–Humid

in this region. Bermudagrass grows throughout this region. Zoysiagras is better adapted to the northern part of it; St. Augustinegrass, bahiagrass, and centipedegrass do better along the Gulf Coast. In the mountainous sections, cool-season grasses will grow.

Transition zone

The Transition Zone covers parts of all four regions. It has hot summers, cold winters, and wet and dry periods throughout the year. Here you can grow either cool- or warm-season grasses but neither does well. Both are on the edge of their adaptation.

Only the grasses that tolerate extremes do well in the Transition Zone. These include tall fescue, a cool-season grass that is better suited to hot summers than most of the other cool-season grasses and can survive the winter in most of the

Transition Zone. Of the warm-season grasses, cold-tolerant varieties of bermudagrass do well in the southern part of the zone; and zoysiagrass grows farther north but is

brown for much of the year. Kentucky bluegrass and perennial ryegrass, or a mix of these two with tall fescue, are a successful mixture for the cooler parts of this zone.

Warm-season grasses, such as St. Augustinegrass, left, grow vigorously and stay green during the heat of summer. During cool weather, they go dormant. A lawn overseeded with ryegrass, right, will stay green all through the winter.

Classes of Grasses *(continued)*

Creeping grasses, such as Kentucky bluegrass, above, spread quickly by stolons or rhizomes.

Bunchgrasses grow in slowly spreading clumps. Mixes of bunchgrasses and creeping grasses often become weedy looking.

Both warm-season and cool-season grasses can be further categorized by the way they grow and by their life span and appearance.

Growth habits: bunching and creeping

Turfgrasses employ two distinct means of spreading: tillering and creeping. Bunchgrasses, such as annual and perennial ryegrass, blue gramagrass, and tall fescue, expand by growing tillers from their crowns. A bunchgrass lawn is a collection of individual plants growing in tufts or bunches.

Creeping grasses, such as bentgrass, Kentucky bluegrass, and Bermudagrass, spread by sending out rhizomes and stolons. Creeping grasses exhibit some tiller growth but expand primarily with creeping stems that root and give rise to new plants. Consequently, a lawn of creeping grass is a thickly knit mat of parent and offspring plants.

Virtually all warm-season grasses are creeping grasses. Their extensive root system helps them survive the stress of heat and drought.

The cool-season category includes bunchgrasses and creeping grasses, and the two types are often combined in northern grass seed mixtures and lawns.

Perennial and annual

Most of the commonly grown turfgrasses are perennial. They live and continue to grow and spread year after year. They may slip into dormancy during the winter and during times of stress from drought or cold, but they spring back to life and resume growing vigorously when weather conditions improve.

Annual grasses live for just one season. There are only a few annual turfgrasses, the most notable being annual ryegrass.

Although annual grasses, especially annual ryegrass, are often used as a component in inexpensive grass seed mixes, they have little value in a permanent lawn. However, because they germinate and grow quickly, they can be used as a temporary lawn. In mild-winter areas, turf growers often use them to overseed the dormant warm-season grasses for winter color.

Texture: fine and coarse

Grasses can also be categorized by their blade width. Those with blades that measure ¼ inch or narrower are known as fine-textured grasses; they form the basis for a good-looking, refined lawn. They include creeping red bentgrass, Kentucky bluegrass, Bermudagrass, and zoysiagrass.

Grasses with blades wider than ¼ inch are called coarse or rough textured. Some of these grasses, such as tall fescue, buffalograss, and varieties of perennial ryegrass, are not far removed in appearance from their pasture-grass parentage. With good maintenance, these grasses form attractive lawns. However, they don't suit everyone's taste.

Over the years, turfgrass breeders have worked to improve the texture of many of these coarse varieties. Not

Blade width can vary considerably among turfgrass species, as shown by the blades of, from left to right, tall fescue, fine fescue, Kentucky bluegrass, and perennial ryegrass.

long ago, for example, tall fescue existed only as a very coarse-bladed grass. But new varieties, known as turf-type tall fescues, have fine blades rivaling those of Kentucky bluegrass.

There is another aesthetic quality of grasses that we look for but do not categorize: color. In our current culture, we favor deep green lawns, the greener the better. That's a benefit of feeding lawns regularly. Color also is genetically determined; some species are naturally a much deeper green color than others. And breeders are taking advantage of that fact to develop new dark-green varieties.

Practical Considerations

ESTABLISHMENT: Bunchgrasses spread more slowly than most creeping grasses and are usually sown at a heavier rate to compensate. Creeping grasses grown from plugs or sprigs, such as hybrid Bermudagrass and zoysiagrass, are slow spreaders too. They may take a full season or longer to cover the ground. Be vigilant about keeping the lawn free of weeds until these grasses become fully established.

WEAR TOLERANCE: In general, bunchgrasses are more durable, resisting wear and tear. If your family is hard on a lawn, using it for football games and other such activities, a bunchgrass such as perennial ryegrass or turf-type tall fescue may be best. However, creeping grasses often recover from injury more quickly.

PERMANENCE: Your lawn should consist almost entirely of blends of perennial grasses. But annual ryegrass can provide a temporary cover until your permanent lawn can be sown or sodded. In winter, you can also seed annual ryegrass over dormant warm-season grasses for all-season color.

AESTHETICS: Texture considerations are primarily aesthetic. Some coarse-textured grasses make a lawn look rough, especially if mixed with finer-textured varieties. Others, such as St. Augustinegrass and tall fescue, are widely used in highly aesthetic situations. If you expect your lawn to be a showcase, and if your patch of turf is more often viewed than used, choose a fine-bladed creeping grass such as Kentucky bluegrass.

Gallery of Grasses

Growing the right grass in the right place is the most important step in making a fine lawn. Turfgrass species vary considerably in climatic, environmental, and cultural preferences. Chances are there's one that's just right for your lawn, or for a troublesome corner of it.

Maybe you're concerned about the grass variety you're growing now. Maybe another species would do better. In either case, whether you're improving your care program to match your lawn or starting a new lawn, you'll benefit from the information in this Gallery of Grasses. You'll find

clues to help you identify the major grass species, and discussions of their strengths and weaknesses, as well as variety recommendations.

We start with cool-season grasses and continue with warm season species on page 28.

Note: Lawn grass seed is rarely packaged as a single species; instead, it's sold as mixtures and blends (see page 45). When buying seed, make sure the label indicates that the bag contains improved cultivars.

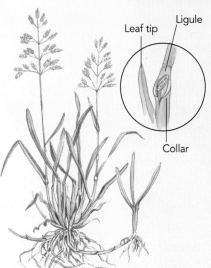

Leaf tip
Ligule
Collar

Blade: V-shaped; boat-shaped tip.
Ligule: Clear, cropped.
Collar: Smooth, yellowish green.
New leaf: Folded.

Poa BLUEGRASS
PO-ah

KENTUCKY BLUEGRASS (*Poa pratensis*) is a cool-season, creeping, fine-textured perennial with good color and vigorous spreading ability. Its appearance is the standard against which all other turfgrasses are measured.

Bluegrass was one of the first turfgrasses to be grown in the early lawns of America, and today it is widely used for lawns, parks, athletic fields, golf fairways, and general-purpose turf. Very cold tolerant, it is best adapted to the northern states east of the Rockies and to the Pacific Northwest, but it also is widely grown in the cool areas and higher elevations of the South. (The Plains states are often too dry for a satisfactory bluegrass lawn.)

Kentucky bluegrass has unjustly acquired the reputation of being a

high-maintenance grass. It's true that the older, common Kentucky bluegrass and some of the older improved varieties were prone to disease. They required high inputs of fertilizer and water to maintain their green color through the growing season. New cultivars, however, have

GROWING BLUEGRASS

KENTUCKY BLUEGRASS
- Mow at 1½-2½ inches.
- Feed three to five times per year.

ROUGH BLUEGRASS
- Mow at 2-3 inches.
- Feed two or three times per year.

CANADA BLUEGRASS
- Mow at 3-4 inches.
- Feed two or three times per year

PROS AND CONS

Kentucky bluegrass is perhaps the cold hardiest of all turfgrasses, making a dependable lawn in the northern reaches of the United States. Wherever it grows, it's noted for its fine texture and dense, thick turf. Though new varieties have some drought tolerance, Kentucky bluegrass requires regular watering to maintain its bright color through hot, dry seasons. It also needs more fertilizing and more frequent mowing than many other cool-season grasses. Kentucky bluegrass was once considered disease prone and intolerant of shade, but most new varieties have good resistance, and some have good shade tolerance as well.

Rough bluegrass grows well in shade but does not tolerate full sun and drought.

Canada bluegrass survives in infertile and acid soils, high elevations, and cool temperatures. It can go for long periods without mowing. However, this species is not suited for fine turf.

good disease resistance and retain their fine appearance without heavy fertilization and watering. New hybrids of Kentucky bluegrass and Texas bluegrass promise to be much more heat and drought tolerant.

ROUGH BLUEGRASS (*Poa trivialis*) is a bright green, fine-textured, shallow-rooted relative of Kentucky bluegrass. Although it is not as versatile as its high-class cousin, it is sometimes used as a substitute in moist soils and shade. The grass is soft bladed, and in mild climates it retains its color over the winter.

Because it can survive without full sun, it is an occasional component in some shady-lawn mixtures.

In the South, it is often used successfully to overseed warm-season grasses to provide winter color.

CANADA BLUEGRASS (*P. compressa*) is a cold-tolerant, creeping, fine-textured bluegrass. As its botanical name suggests, it can be identified by its flattened stems.

Its common name gives a clue to its natural growing range: It is well-adapted to Canada and the northern United States.

Planted as a low-maintenance turf, Canada bluegrass can survive even in very poor soil. Although this species was once considered a lawn weed because it tends to form thin turf, new cultivars demonstrate better density and vigor. Canada bluegrass is sometimes substituted for higher-maintenance turf in conservation areas, on banks, and in hard-to-access areas.

ANNUAL BLUEGRASS (*P. annua*), a low-growing, creeping grass, is a weed. Avoid any seed mixtures containing it.

Kentucky bluegrass

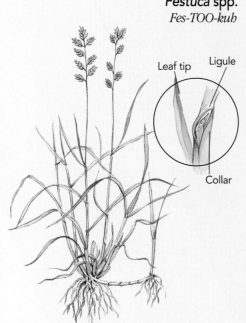

Festuca spp.
Fes-TOO-kuh

Leaf tip   Ligule

Collar

Blade: Folded; boat-shaped tip.
Ligule: Clear, short.
Collar: Smooth.
New leaf: Folded.

FINE FESCUES

Fine fescues, which include chewings, hard, red (sometimes called creeping red), and sheep fescues, are fine-bladed grasses. They are used extensively in seed blends and mixes for both sunny and shady situations.

Some fine fescue varieties germinate and become established quickly. They are medium green in color. Some spread by tillers, others by short, creeping rhizomes. Fine fescues don't like heat; during extended hot, dry periods, they may lose their color rapidly.

Though members of this family behave similarly, there are differences among them.

CHEWINGS FESCUE (*Festuca rubra commutata*) is an aggressive, bunch-type fine fescue that can overtake other grasses. That's good for crowding out weeds but not for maintaining other grasses. It is sometimes used to overseed shady lawns, often in mixtures with perennial ryegrass or Kentucky bluegrass.

Chewings fescue is adapted to cooler areas in the northern United States and Canada and to the coastal regions of the Northeast and Pacific Northwest. Elsewhere it is best suited to areas where summers are cool.

Because it is moderately wear tolerant and well-adapted to sandy,

PROS AND CONS

Chewings fescue is among the most shade tolerant of cool-season grasses. It is susceptible to disease when the weather is hot and wet, and it does not withstand heavy use well.

Hard fescue is shade and salt tolerant and drought resistant. It requires less mowing and less fertilizer than other fescues, and it is highly resistant to many diseases. Its wearability is not especially good, and some older varieties are difficult to mow evenly, the blade tips becoming shredded and discolored.

Red fescue is very shade and drought tolerant, but it takes less heat than other fescues. It is susceptible to summer diseases in hot climates.

Sheep fescue is tolerant of a wide variety of soil types and can take partial shade, but it does not make a smooth turf.

acid, and infertile soils in these regions, chewings fescue is a good choice for a low-maintenance turf in shaded, low-traffic areas in parks and lawns.

HARD FESCUE (*F. longifolia*) is a fine-textured grass grown mostly at high elevations in the northern United States and Canada.

It has gained popularity lately as a strong, low-maintenance grass. It requires low fertilization, and its short growth and slow growth rate mean less frequent mowings.

Growing in clumps, hard fescue is slower to become established than chewings fescue and red fescue, but it needs minimal maintenance when mature. It has narrow, firm leaves. It does not form rhizomes, making it somewhat less resistant to wear. It is very well-suited to covering slopes and banks.

RED FESCUE (*F. rubra*), also known as creeping red fescue, is often

CHEWINGS FESCUE AND RED FESCUE
- Mow at 1½–2½ inches.
- Feed two or three times per year.

HARD FESCUE
- Mow at 1½–2½ inches, or leave unmown in conservation areas.
- Feed two or three times per year.

SHEEP FESCUE
- Mow at 2–4 inches, or leave unmown in conservation areas.
- Feed two or three times per year (feeding can be reduced in low-maintenance areas).

combined with Kentucky bluegrass in good-quality lawn seed mixes. A fine-textured, low-maintenance grass with narrow dark green blades, it blends well and does what most bluegrasses cannot—it grows well in shade and drought. It is preferable to chewings fescue in a seed mix because it is more wear tolerant and is less likely to form thatch.

Red fescue has a creeping growth habit, spreading by rhizomes and tillers. It is best adapted where summers are cool, such as in the coastal Northwest and at high elevations, and it is widely planted in the Great Lakes region.

Growing well on banks and slopes, red fescue creates an especially lush effect when left unmowed. It is also good for overseeding dormant warm-season grasses in winter, provided that the site isn't heavily trafficked.

SHEEP FESCUE (*F. ovina*) is a cool-season perennial bunchgrass that requires little water. Once established, it is persistent and winter hardy.

Though it does not make an elegant lawn, sheep fescue is a good low-maintenance grass for off-the-beaten-path areas in public parks and lawns. Improved varieties have finely textured deep blue-green foliage.

Sheep fescue does well in cool, dry areas and requires infrequent mowing and minimal fertilizer.

Fine fescue

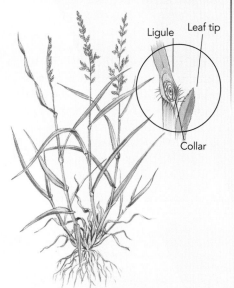

Festuca arundinacea
fess-TOO-kuh ah-run-din-AY-cee-ah

Ligule
Leaf tip
Collar

Blade: Broad, flat; blunt tip.
Ligule: Clear, long, cropped.
Collar: Hairy.
New leaf: Rolled.

TALL FESCUE

Tall fescue, a dense clumping grass that is able to grow in sun or shade and is a good low-maintenance choice for home lawns, playing fields, and commercial grounds. It performs best in areas with mild winters and warm summers and in mild-temperature regions of the Southwest. It's one of the best turf choices for the Transition Zone. Where winters are mild, it will stay green all year.

Until recently, tall fescue was considered a poor grass for a good-looking lawn. The few available cultivars of tall fescue were coarse and pale colored, and they did not stand up well to wear. During the past several years, however, breeders have worked wonders with this species, and the new turf-type tall fescue varieties exhibit fine lawn qualities: good appearance, wearability, and moderate fertilizer requirements. Several of the turf-type tall fescues have fine-textured blades and good, rich color, as opposed to their coarser precursors.

Turf-type tall fescues tolerate high and infrequent mowing. Many of these varieties also demonstrate good disease and drought tolerance. Some even resist damage from insects.

GROWING FESCUE

- Mow at 2½–3 inches.
- Feed two to four times per year (four times in areas with long growing seasons).

PROS AND CONS

Tall fescues prefer high mowing. In some areas, they grow rapidly in spring. New varieties stay green throughout the growing season with little fertilizer. Most are drought tolerant. Those qualities make tall fescue a good choice for low-maintenance lawns. However, most tall fescues do not mix well with other grasses, with the exception of nonaggressive bluegrass varieties. Older varieties of fescue such as 'Kentucky 31' and 'Alta' are light colored and coarse textured, creating a weedy appearance to lawns with fine turfgrasses.

Tall fescue

PERENNIAL RYEGRASS exhibits the best wear tolerance of any cool-season grass, which is why it's commonly selected to plant on playing fields and well-used home lawns. Like tall fescue, it has received a lot of attention from turf breeders. The result has been new, moderate- to high-maintenance turf-type perennial ryegrass varieties that are fine bladed, rich green, and resistant to pests and diseases.

Blade: Flat; sharp tip.
Ligule: Clear, long, cropped.
Collar: Narrow.
New leaf: Folded.

PROS AND CONS

Perennial ryegrass is a good low-maintenance choice for home lawns subject to a lot of wear and traffic. It can be mowed closely or left to grow long. New varieties have more insect resistance than any other species but require a higher level of maintenance. Perennial ryegrass does not do well in shade, extreme cold, or heat and drought. Annual ryegrass germinates extremely quickly and can be used to establish temporary lawns.

RYEGRASS

Perennial ryegrass can be grown successfully throughout the cool-season turfgrass regions and in cooler parts and higher elevations of the warm-season regions. It is not as cold tolerant as Kentucky bluegrass or as drought tolerant as tall fescue.

Perennial ryegrass likes full sun but will tolerate some shade. Its bunch-type growth forms a uniform lawn if it is properly maintained. **ANNUAL RYEGRASS** *(Lolium multiflorum),* also known as Italian ryegrass, is a cool-season annual grass that forms a medium- to coarse-textured lawn with moderate wear resistance. Though seed of annual rye is often found in inexpensive grass mixes, it does not belong in a permanent lawn because it lives for only one year. In temperate areas, it is sometimes used as temporary lawn; in mild-winter areas it is often overseeded on dormant warm-season grasses to provide winter color.

Perennial ryegrass

GROWING RYEGRASS

PERENNIAL RYEGRASS
■ Mow at 1½–2½ inches.
■ Feed three to five times per year

ANNUAL RYEGRASS
■ Mow at 1½–2½ inches.
■ Feed three to five times per year.

Agrostis spp.
uh-GRAHSS-tiss

BENTGRASS

Leaf tip   Ligule

Collar

Blade: Narrow, flat; broadly pointed tip.
Ligule: Clear, pointed, long.
Collar: Narrow.
New leaf: Rolled.

Bentgrass

The bentgrasses are the finest-bladed, lowest-growing, and highest-maintenance species of all the cool-season turfgrasses. It's true they make a fine-looking lawn, but they require a great deal of care—frequent mowing, watering, and fertilizing.

Their distinctive growth habit and color do not mix well with other grasses. They are susceptible to many diseases. On the positive side, there are species well-adapted to small regions of the country where they can survive with less care.

CREEPING BENTGRASS *(Agrostis palustris)* is fine textured and low growing. This is a grass that's used on putting and bowling greens. It forms a soft, dense, carpetlike lawn but requires good drainage and frequent watering. It also requires good airflow over the surface of the lawn to prevent disease. It will tolerate some shade but does better in full sun.

COLONIAL BENTGRASS *(A. tenuis)* is a bit more user-friendly. It tolerates higher mowing and less fertilizer. When mowed closely, it forms a dense turf. If left unmown, it can serve as a conservation grass, stabilizing banks. It is well-adapted to the Pacific Northwest.

VELVET BENTGRASS *(A. canina)* is the finest textured of all the bentgrasses. It is frequently used on golf courses and putting greens because it makes a fine, dense turf that can be mowed quite short. Velvet bentgrass is lighter in color than other bentgrasses. It grows best in the northern United States, especially in coastal areas where it is cool and moist and soils are fertile.

GROWING BENTGRASS

■ Mow frequently at ½–¾ inch.
■ Feed three to five times per year.
■ Dethatch regularly.

PROS AND CONS

Though they make fine-looking lawns and are tolerant of acid soils and light shade, bentgrasses are, for the most part, more trouble than they are worth. They require large amounts of fertilizer, water, and pesticides and frequent mowing and dethatching. The seeds are extremely small, so a well-prepared seedbed is required, and the grass is slow to become established from seed. Colonial bentgrass, however, can serve as a low-maintenance grass in areas of the Pacific Northwest.

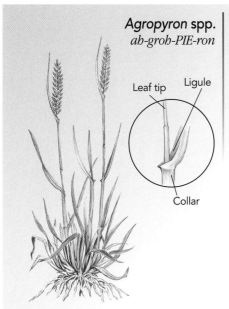

Agropyron spp.
ah-groh-PIE-ron

Leaf tip   Ligule

Collar

Blade: Stiff, erect, ribbed.
Ligule: Clear.
Collar: Broad.
New leaf: Rolled.

PROS AND CONS

Wheatgrass shows promise as a lawn grass in the northern Great Plains and intermountain region. Tough and durable, wheatgrass is able to survive drought and very cold winter conditions. It needs little watering and if it turns brown from lack of moisture, it will green up quickly if watered.

Wheatgrass also requires less fertilizer than other lawn grasses. It makes a decent turfgrass and wears well when not mown too short.

Wheatgrass is coarse textured and does not form a dense, tight turf. It also goes dormant in hot weather. It is best considered as an alternative lawn for a specific geographic area.

WHEATGRASS

Wheatgrass is a cool-season grass, some species of which are native to the arid plains of the upper Midwest and the intermountain region. Conventional lawn grasses have a difficult time in the harsh conditions of the plains, and adapting tough native grasses to lawn use can provide an alternative lawn. A wheatgrass lawn looks rather different from traditional lawns, but it requires less care and is better able to survive the growing conditions without stress. Wheatgrass has long been used as a forage and pasture grass and is grown for hay. It can also be adapted for lawn use if it is not mown too closely. It is quite drought tolerant but tends to go dormant in hot weather. Watering will bring it back if browning occurs. Wheatgrass is sometimes used in Montana, South Dakota, North Dakota, Wyoming, and central Canada.

There are several species of wheatgrass, all of which are very winter hardy. Here are three of them.

CRESTED WHEATGRASS (*Agropyron sibiricum*), native to Eurasia and introduced to North America, is a perennial bunchgrass that establishes easily. The leaves are bluish green and coarse textured. In a lawn for a sunny, dry location, crested wheatgrass can be used by itself or mixed with smooth brome and western wheatgrass. It can also be used for erosion control on slopes. It needs less fertilizer than conventional turfgrasses and can withstand long dry periods. Crested wheatgrass puts on most of its growth in spring and fall.

FAIRWAY WHEATGRASS (*A. cristatum*) was introduced to North America from Siberia. It is a bright green perennial bunchgrass that is shorter and finer stemmed than crested wheatgrass. Its dense growth and reasonably fine texture make it acceptable as a lawn. Like other wheatgrasses, fairway wheatgrass tolerates drought; it also tolerates poor soil as long as the soil is dry.

Fairway wheatgrass in North Dakota

This is the type of wheatgrass most often used for lawns.

WESTERN WHEATGRASS (*A. smithii*), the state grass of North Dakota, is a rhizomatous, sod-forming species native to the plains. It has blue-green leaves and low to medium density. Western wheatgrass is long lived and tolerates alkaline conditions. It is drought resistant but also withstands periodic flooding.

GROWING WHEATGRASS

■ If grass turns brown in summer, water to reinvigorate it.
■ Mow at 2–2½ inches. Wheatgrass wears best when it is not mown too closely.
■ Feed one to three times per year.

BUFFALOGRASS

Buchloe dactyloides
buk-LO-ee dak-til-OY-deez

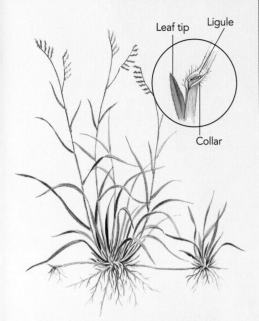

Leaf tip   Ligule

Collar

Blade: Flat, gray-green, hairy.
Ligule: Long hairs.
Collar: Broad, smooth.
New leaf: Rolled.

A North American native grass sometimes grown as turf, buffalograss has fine-textured, curling blades with outstanding heat tolerance. Gray-green from late spring to hard frost, this warm-season grass turns straw color through its dormancy in late fall and winter. It does well in heavy soil but prefers finer-textured soils. Occasionally planted for its low maintenance, buffalograss thrives

PROS AND CONS

Though it needs little or no irrigation, fertilization, or watering, buffalograss does not meet everyone's expectations of a lawn. It makes a matted, reasonably dense turf, and newer varieties have a good soft green color.

Though buffalograss is highly drought- and heat-resistant, many cultivars turn brown in extremely hot or cold temperatures. However, buffalograss can be mown like turfgrass and is becoming more popular in arid areas.

A lawn of mown buffalograss

in areas that receive only 12 to 25 inches of rain per year. This includes the region that stretches from Minnesota to central Montana and south from Minnesota to Iowa, parts of Texas, and into northern Mexico.

Once one of the dominant grasses of the American prairie, buffalograss forms a matted, fine-textured, reasonably dense turf that greens up early in spring, takes hard wear, and looks good with little summer watering. It is best adapted to drier areas where other grasses and weeds are unable to compete with it. It suffers when overwatered. More lawnlike in appearance than other native grasses, it is becoming increasingly popular in drought-prone regions. Given plenty of sun and minimal watering, it grows slowly to 4 to 6 inches tall and requires little or no mowing. All-female varieties have no pollen and are well-tolerated by allergy sufferers; these varieties are available as sod or, in some cases, plugs.

GROWING BUFFALOGRASS

- Sow 2 pounds of seed per 1,000 square feet; or plant 2-inch plugs at 1-foot intervals.
- Mow at 2–3 inches if a conventional turf is desired; otherwise, leave unmown.
- Feed one or two times per year.

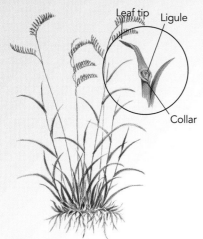

Bouteloua gracilis
boo-tell-OO-ah grah-SEE-liss

Leaf tip Ligule

Collar

Blade: Flat, hairy; broadly pointed tip.
Ligule: Short hairs.
Collar: Broad, hairy.
New leaf: Rolled.

GROWING BLUE GRAMAGRASS

- Sow 2–4 pounds of seed per 1,000 square feet.
- Mow at 2–3 inches, or leave unmown.
- Feed once or twice per year.

BLUE GRAMAGRASS

Blue gramagrass is another native of the prairies of the Great Plains. For years, it has been used as a pasture or conservation grass. However, it is sometimes put to use on lawns because it can take mowing and serve as low-maintenance turf. It needs just 10 inches of rainfall a year. Blue gramagrass is sometimes mixed with buffalograss seed to improve its appearance.

Grayish green with fine-textured, curling leaves, blue gramagrass has excellent pest and disease resistance and tolerance to heat, cold, drought, and alkaline soils. Although technically a warm-season grass, it remains hardy to minus 40° F. It adapts to sandy soils and tolerates alkaline conditions.

This grass spreads by short stolons and produces hairy leaves that grow in low tufts. Blue gramagrass can be left unmown or, for a more turflike appearance, mowed three or four times per year. Two varieties, 'Hachita' and 'Lovington', are produced principally for use on rangelands, but they also are suitable for low-maintenance prairie-style lawns.

PROS AND CONS

Though extremely drought- and heat-resistant, blue gramagrass (which is gray-green in color) turns brown in hot, dry weather. It does not form a thick turf. Because it germinates and establishes slowly, give it a head start—sow in early spring or in fall.

Blue gramagrass

Cynodon spp.
SI-no-don

Leaf tip   Ligule

Collar

Blade: Rough; pointed tip.
Ligule: White hairs.
Collar: Narrow, smooth.
New leaf: Folded.

BERMUDAGRASS

Bermudagrass is to the southern United States what Kentucky bluegrass is to the North—the stuff of which most lawns are made.

This creeping turfgrass is easily grown in most soils and takes both low- and high-maintenance regimes. Depending on the variety, Bermudagrass resists many diseases and can take considerable wear and abuse. Deep roots allow it to tolerate heat and drought (although a Bermudagrass lawn always looks better when it receives adequate water).

Bermudagrass grows throughout the warm-season turfgrass area and well into some areas of the cool-season region. However, it is best adapted to lower elevations in the Southwest and in a region bounded by Maryland,

PROS AND CONS

Bermudagrass is a good-looking, dense, hardworking lawn for most of the South. It stands up to wear and tear and hot summer weather. However, Bermudagrass's aggressive nature can work against it. It spreads by means of aggressive runners into flower beds, sidewalk cracks, etcetera. Bermudagrass is a relatively heavy feeder and often requires irrigation to retain its color. Feeding and watering, in turn, increase the mowing required during the summer. Bermudagrass may turn yellow if allowed to grow too tall.

Florida, Texas, and Kansas. When Bermudagrass invades cool-season turf, it is considered a weed.

Older, common Bermudagrass can be difficult to contain and keep out of areas where it is not wanted, such as flower borders and beds. Its vigorous growth rate also makes it prone to thatching, and it is subject to damage from insects and diseases.

It does not grow well in shade and often goes dormant, turning yellow or brown, when fall temperatures drop to the range of 50–60° F. Bermudagrass has been much improved in recent years, with new hybrid varieties that show improved texture and color and tolerance to drought, heat, and cold.

Softer, denser, and finer textured than common Bermudagrass, hybrid varieties are fast-growing, durable, heat-loving grasses used for sites from home lawns to golf courses. However, hybrid Bermudagrass needs more sun, more fertilizer, and more frequent mowing than its common cousins. In fact, hybrid Bermudagrass lawns should be mowed twice a week during their peak growth period in summer.

Many hybrid Bermudagrass seeds are sterile, so the turfgrass must be propagated by sod, sprigs, or stolons. However, some improved seeded varieties are available.

GROWING BERMUDAGRASS

COMMON BERMUDAGRASS
■ Mow often at ½-2 inches.
■ Feed four to six times per year.

HYBRID BERMUDAGRASS
■ Plant 2-inch sprigs 12 inches apart or 2 bushels of sprigs per 1,000 square feet.

■ Mow at ½-2 inches as often as twice weekly during peak growth periods.
■ Feed four to six times per year.

Bermudagrass

Paspalum notatum
pass-PAL-uhm NO-tah-tum

Ligule
Leaf tip
Collar

BAHIAGRASS

Bahiagrass is a tough, coarse-textured, moderately aggressive warm-season grass that is adapted to a wide range of soil conditions. Although it grows well in an area that stretches from the central coast of North Carolina, south to central and southern Florida, and west to eastern Texas, it is generally used on the Gulf Coast of Florida.

Bahiagrass spreads slowly by short rhizomes. It becomes aggressive when established, quickly making a thick, low-maintenance turf. It has some drought resistance.

Because of its coarse blades and uneven growth, Bahiagrass does not make an especially good-looking lawn, and the tough stems are difficult to mow evenly. Older, common Bahiagrass is the coarsest of all and is susceptible to damage below 20° F. Newer varieties are more cold tolerant and not as coarse.

Blades: Flat or folded.
Ligule: Clear, cropped.
Collar: Broad.
New leaf: Rolled.

SEASHORE PASPALUM
(P. vaginatum), a related variety, is a fine-textured Bahiagrass that grows naturally in coastal environments and is tolerant of salty soils and poor-quality water.

PROS AND CONS

Bahiagrass is somewhat shade and drought tolerant and forms a thick turf that crowds out weeds without creating thatch. It grows well in sandy, slightly acid, infertile soil. However, bahiagrass needs frequent mowing to maintain its good looks and is susceptible to brown patch, dollar spot, and mole crickets.

GROWING BAHIAGRASS

■ Sow 6-10 pounds of seed per 1,000 square feet or propagate by sprigs or sod.
■ Mow frequently at 2-4 inches.
■ Feed two to four times per year.

Bahiagrass

Zoysia spp.
ZOY-zhuh

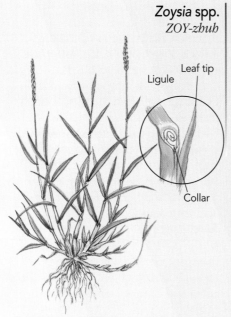

Leaf tip
Ligule
Collar

Blade: Flat, stiff, hairy; pointed tip.
Ligule: Short hairs.
Collar: Broad, hairy.
New leaf: Rolled.

ZOYSIAGRASS

Zoysiagrass is a tough, aggressive, creeping warm-season perennial with leaf texture that ranges from coarse to fine, depending on variety.

This grass is often advertised as a miracle grass. It has some outstanding characteristics. Tolerant of heat and drought yet able to endure some shade and cool temperatures, zoysiagrass forms a dense, wiry, low-maintenance lawn that crowds out weeds. However, the needlelike blades of many zoysiagrass cultivars can be sharp underfoot, and it tends to form a puffy turf. Zoysiagrass grows slowly and takes longer to establish than many other turfgrasses. Some varieties tolerate low water, but zoysiagrass is less drought tolerant than Bermudagrass.

Zoysiagrass is sometimes grown in the Transition Zone between warm- and cool-season areas, and as far north as New Jersey in the East and Oregon in the West. In these areas it is at its best in summer and competes well with warm-season weeds such as crabgrass. It will survive winters, but at the first hint of cold weather, it goes dormant and turns brown, whereas cool-season grasses are still bright green. It is also slow to green in the spring; in most of the Transition Zone it is brown from October through April.

Three species are available. *Zoysia japonica* is the hardiest and most vigorous, but its leaves are the coarsest. *Z. matrella* is not as hardy or coarse. It is wear resistant and tolerates some shade. *Z. tenuifolia* is the least hardy but is the finest textured and the most attractive.

Older cultivars could not be propagated from seed, and lawns had to be started vegetatively from plugs. However, new, improved varieties may be grown from seed.

GROWING ZOYSIAGRASS

■ Sow 1–2 pounds of hulled seed per 1,000 square feet (or plant 2-inch plugs 6 inches apart). Keep lawn weed free.
■ Mow at ½–2 inches.
■ Feed three to five times per year.

PROS AND CONS

Zoysiagrass forms a dense turf that is resistant to weeds, insects, and diseases.

It does not aggressively invade garden beds, as does Bermudagrass. However, it establishes slowly, browns out early in fall, and is slow to green up in spring.

Zoysiagrass does not mix well with other grasses in a lawn. Fine-leaved varieties tend toward a "fluffy" growth that often looks scalped when mown.

Zoysiagrass

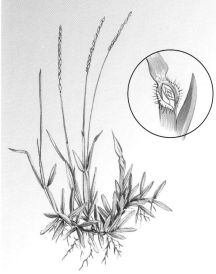

Eremochloa ophiuroides
Err-ri-MOCK-low-uh OH-fie-uhr-OY-deez

Blade: Flat; boat-shaped tip.
Ligule: Clear, purplish.
Collar: Hairy, cinched.
New leaf: Folded.

CENTIPEDEGRASS

Centipedegrass, a coarse-textured light green grass that spreads by way of leafy stolons, is sometimes called "lazy man's grass" because of its low maintenance requirements. It needs less mowing than other grasses, and it adapts to poor soil, resists chinch bugs and brown patch disease, and is aggressive enough to crowd out weeds. These qualities make it an excellent choice for general-purpose lawns in the Southeast and Gulf Coast states.

Centipedegrass has shallow roots and only moderate drought tolerance. It is often the first warm-season grass to turn brown in hot, dry periods. 'Oaklawn' is an improved variety, with greater drought and cold tolerance.

Also sensitive to low temperatures, centipedegrass tends to go dormant when cold. It turns green again when temperatures warm up. However, extended periods of temperatures below 5° F can kill centipedegrass. It will not withstand much traffic and is slow to recover when damaged.

Centipedegrass should not be planted near beach areas because it cannot tolerate salt spray. It is particularly sensitive to iron deficiencies, which can arise in alkaline soils.

GROWING CENTIPEDEGRASS

■ Sow common centipedegrass seed at a rate of 1–2 pounds per 1,000 square feet. Plant sprigs or sod plugs of other varieties on 1-foot centers. Water thoroughly when centipedegrass shows signs of stress: wilted and discolored leaves. Apply iron sulfate if chlorosis appears.
■ Mow at 1–3 inches.
■ Feed two times per year.

PROS AND CONS

Centipedegrass is a relatively fine-bladed, dense-growing turfgrass that thrives in sandy, acid soils and requires low fertility. It grows slowly, so it needs less frequent mowing than Bermudagrass. However, it is susceptible to hard freezes, may require extra iron, and does not tolerate heavy wear.

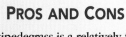

Centipedegrass

Stenotaphrum secundatum
STEHN-oh-taff-rum sebk-un-DOT-um

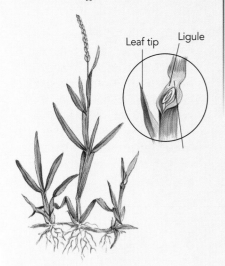

Leaf tip   Ligule

Blade: Flat, smooth; blunt.
Ligule: Short hairs.
Collar: Broad, smooth.
New leaf: Folded.

St. Augustinegrass

St. Augustinegrass is a robust, fast-growing, coarse-textured, warm-season perennial with broad dark green blades. It spreads by means of stolons that root at the nodes and form a thick, dense turf that crowds out most weeds. Suitable for lawns where a fine texture is not required, St. Augustinegrass is among the most shade tolerant of warm-season grasses. It is adapted to Southern California, Hawaii, Texas, and other mild areas of the Southwest as well as Florida and other Gulf Coast states. St. Augustinegrass withstands heat well and is tolerant of salt spray and salty soil. It withstands drought moderately well but performs best with weekly watering. It tends to lose its color as soon as the weather turns cold.

St. Augustinegrass

St. Augustinegrass is not low maintenance. It requires a fertile soil, well drained, and rich in organic matter. Even in good soil, it requires regular fertilization with a high-nitrogen fertilizer. It is also susceptible to insect damage and diseases, including the viral St. Augustinegrass decline (SAD). Improved varieties offer resistance to disease and insect damage.

In spring and fall, St. Augustinegrass lawns grow slowly and require only twice-monthly mowing. During peak summer

Pros and Cons

St. Augustinegrass forms a thick turf that crowds out weeds, stands up to wear, and tolerates shade, heat, salty soil, and moderate cold. New varieties are more cold tolerant and tend to hold their green color longer than Bermudagrass.

St. Augustinegrass requires high fertilizer levels and regular watering, and its subsequent rapid growth often leads to a buildup of thatch, which must be removed regularly.

St. Augustinegrass

growth, lawns must be mowed at least weekly. Proper mowing height is critical. If mowed too low, weeds may get an upper hand. If allowed to grow too high between mowings, thatch may build up.

St. Augustinegrass does not produce viable seed, so it must be planted by sprigs or sod. Because of its dense growth, St. Augustinegrass forms a springy turf that is prone to thatch, which must be removed regularly to allow moisture and fertilizer to penetrate the soil.

GROWING ST. AUGUSTINEGRASS

- Plant 3- to 4-inch sod plugs at 1-foot intervals anytime during the growing season, as long as you can provide adequate water. During slow growth in spring and fall, keep the lawn free of weeds while it becomes established.
- Mow regularly at 2–4 inches.

- Feed four or five times per year.
- Applications of ferrous sulfate or chelated iron will enhance the appearance of St. Augustinegrass and help prevent chlorosis or yellowing of the leaves. High-quality turf fertilizers contain sufficient iron.

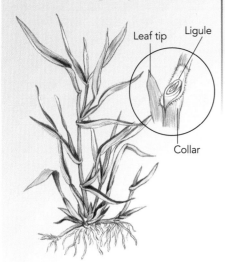

Axonopus fissifolius
AXE-oh-nop-uss fiss-ee-FOL-ee-us

Leaf tip
Ligule
Collar

Blade: Smooth; sharp tip.
Ligule: Long hairs.
Collar: Narrow, smooth.
New leaf: Folded.

GROWING CARPETGRASS

- Sow 5-10 pounds of seed per 1,000 square feet, or plant sprigs 6-12 inches apart in rows 12 inches apart.
- Mow every 10–14 days at 1 inch.
- Feed one to three times per year.

CARPETGRASS

Carpetgrass is a specialized creeping grass that forms a dense, fast-growing, wear-tolerant turf. It grows well in the lower coastal plains of the United States.

It does not make an especially attractive lawn and is seldom used anymore. Its blades are coarse, and the plant forms unattractive seed heads if allowed to grow more than an inch tall. Frequent mowing is a must to keep it below that height. However, if maintained well, carpetgrass is a disease- and insect-tolerant turfgrass that stands up to heavy wear.

This grass grows vigorously in sandy, acid soils, even without additional fertilization. However, drought tolerance is not one of its strengths. In areas with infrequent rainfall, it must be irrigated regularly.

Carpetgrass is also cold sensitive and cannot survive winter temperatures much north of central Georgia and North Carolina. Even in the Deep South, it will go dormant and turn brown during the relatively cooler winter months.

Native to the Gulf Coast, it grows best from Texas to Florida and north to Virginia. In those areas, it can withstand more shade and moisture than Bermudagrass.

PROS AND CONS

Carpetgrass grows vigorously by creeping stolons to form a dense, wear-tolerant turf that withstands low fertility. However, it has poor drought and cold tolerance. The grass is not attractive: It is light green, coarse textured, and prone to forming seed heads. There are no improved cultivars of carpetgrass.

Carpetgrass

Other Grasses

Some homeowners lack the time and commitment required to maintain a conventional lawn. There are some alternative grasses and grasslike plants, many of them North American natives, that can be planted for lawns in these situations.

A lawn of native grasses requires the same site preparation as a conventional lawn, and the lawn is established with the same techniques. Generally, seeding rates are higher to ensure a dense enough stand of grass for a lawn. Rhizomatous grasses continue to fill in as they grow, but bunchgrasses do not, so it's important to plant the latter thickly. Here are some grasses and grasslike plants to consider for alternative lawns.

Though technically not a grass, dichondra has small bright-green leaves that provide the look of lawn.

Dichondra

Dichondra (*Dichondra micrantha*) is not a grass but a perennial warm-season groundcover with small, round, bright-green leaves. In previous years it was a popular turf substitute in coastal southern California, but today there are no herbicides labeled for controlling weeds in dichondra so it is rarely planted. It requires well-drained soil. Dichondra can be mowed or left unmown, and it tolerates only light to moderate traffic. It is best used for small lawns. Apply fertilizer before planting at 1 pound of nitrogen per 1,000 square feet. Sow in late spring to early summer, when air temperatures are above 70° F. Sow 1 pound per 500 to 1,000 square feet. Keep the seedbed moist but not soggy; do not let it dry out.

Fertilize monthly with a good turf fertilizer. Water deeply once a week. Mow every two weeks to 1½ to 2 inches.

Junegrass

Junegrass (*Koeleria macrantha*) is a cool-season bunchgrass native to the midwestern prairies of the United States and Canada. It has slender medium-green leaves and grows 18 inches high if left unmown. Junegrass thrives in coarse, well-drained soil of low fertility. The best junegrass for lawns is the nonnative cultivar 'Barkoel', which forms a dense, low-growing turf. Sow in early spring at a rate of 2 to 4 pounds per 1,000 square feet. Fertilize at planting time with an all-purpose balanced fertilizer, and do not fertilize again. Overfertilizing can lead to disease problems. Mow every three to four weeks to 3 inches.

Kikuyugrass

Kikuyugrass (*Pennisetum clandestinum*) is a warm-season, sod-forming lawn grass suited to irrigated low-desert areas of the Southwest. It is drought tolerant and forms a dense turf that wears well. Kikuyugrass can substitute for Bermudagrass in parts of the Southwest. It greens up earlier in spring and stays green longer in fall. Kikuyugrass appears not to cause allergy problems in people who are sensitive to Bermudagrass. Sow in early

spring at a rate of 2 to 3 pounds per 1,000 square feet, and fertilize regularly during the growing season with a balanced fertilizer. Mow to a height of 1 to 2 inches.

Needlegrass

Needlegrass (*Nassella* spp.) is a group of native cool-season bunchgrasses that once populated the interior of California. Nodding needlegrass (*N. cernua*) does best in a dry, sunny location; foothill needlegrass (*N. lepida*) grows in sun or partial shade; and purple needlegrass (*N. pulchra*) needs a sunny location with excellent drainage. All are drought tolerant and can take foot traffic when mowed as a lawn. Needlegrasses go dormant in hot weather, but mowing periodically and watering once a month will keep them green. Mow at least two or three times a year.

Sedges

Sedges (*Carex* spp.) are grasslike plants, not true grasses. When used as a lawn, they need little or no mowing (just once a month or two or three times a year) and less fertilizing than traditional turfgrasses; they have a good green color. Sedge lawns are planted from plugs spaced 6 to 12 inches apart.

California meadow sedge (*C. pansa*) tolerates a range of soils in the West and grows best in sun to partial shade. It has a dark-green color and tolerates some heavy traffic.

Pennsylvania sedge (*C. pensylvanica*) grows well in shade and forms a dense mat of medium-green leaves. Mow to 3 to 4 inches.

For a natural-looking lawn that requires less mowing and water, try a mix of native grasses such as sedges, bluestem, and blue gramagrass. Talk to your cooperative extension agent about mixes that have been developed for your region.

Texas hill country sedge (*C. perdentata*) has soft medium-green evergreen leaves and grows well in sun or shade in a range of soils. It can tolerate drought but looks better when watered.

Baltimore sedge (*C. senta*), a good choice for deep shade, is more cold tolerant. Plant plugs 6 to 8 inches apart on center in spring or fall.

Catlin sedge (*C. texensis*) thrives in many climates, from hot and humid to hot and dry, and is hardy as far north as Pennsylvania. Its leaves are dark green, and it grows best in partial to full shade. Plant plugs 6 inches apart.

CHAMOMILE AND THYME LAWNS

Here's an unusual choice for a lawn: fragrant flowering thyme and chamomile. These herbs grow low and will tolerate moderate foot traffic. Their best feature is that every footfall brings forth a heady herbal aroma. They're not practical for large areas—they're more expensive than grass and won't withstand heavy traffic—but consider them for a small area adjoining a lawn or near an herb garden. Just plant seedlings, or sow seeds and water carefully until established.

A lawn of thyme

The Best Lawn for Your Region

A great-looking lawn starts with planting the right grass for your region. Different grasses grow best in different places. Your cousin in Oregon might have a lot of red fescue in the lawn, whereas your brother in Colorado has buffalograss, and you, in Pennsylvania, have a mix of bluegrass and perennial ryegrass. See page 122 for information on how to find out more about your region.

Growing conditions vary within a region and even within a neighborhood. You probably have several different environments (or microclimates) right on your own property. For instance, a location at the bottom of a hill will be cooler, and slower to warm in spring, than a spot higher up because cold air flows down the slope and collects at the bottom. When choosing lawn grasses, you need to be familiar with the growing conditions where the lawn will be. Study the sun/shade patterns from spring to fall and morning to night to know where you will need shade-tolerant grass varieties. Be familiar with how wet or dry your soil is. See pages 54–55 for information on how to analyze your soil.

In this section you will find recommended grass varieties

The Northeast is known for distinct seasons, and each season brings changes in lawns and lawn care.

for your region, guidelines for when to plant, weather conditions that may affect your lawn, maintenance advice, and information on pests and diseases to watch out for.

Northeast

The northeastern part of the country runs from Maine to Maryland, from the eastern seaboard west to Pennsylvania.

The best lawns in the Northeast are generally mixtures of Kentucky bluegrass, perennial ryegrass, and fescues. A fine fescue blend is recommended for shade. All are considered cool-season grasses.

Not all perennial ryegrasses are hardy in northern New England; check with your county extension office for information on varieties suited to your area. In the central part of this region the best lawn grasses include Kentucky

bluegrass, rough bluegrass, perennial ryegrasses, fine fescues, tall fescues, and bentgrasses. Farther south, tall fescue is the best overall lawn grass. Kentucky bluegrass looks great but requires more maintenance. Zoysiagrass works well and is low maintenance in the central and southern parts of the region, but it is slow and expensive to establish and has a shorter growing season, greening up later in spring and going dormant earlier in fall.

When planting a new lawn, take time to improve the soil first. Turfgrasses don't take well to acid soils, so test your soil and, if necessary, spread lime in advance of planting. Depending on the soil's pH, you may need to apply lime yearly after the lawn is established. The best time to plant a lawn is late summer to early fall so it will have two cool growing seasons before

THE NORTHEAST AT A GLANCE

CLIMATE: Temperate, but some hot summer weather; cold winters, especially in northern New England and at higher elevations.
SOILS: Vary, but generally clay except in sandy coastal areas. Soil pH generally mildly acid, though areas that were formerly pine and oak forest are more strongly acid.
MOISTURE: Abundant rainfall, humid summers. Occasional periods of drought.

the stressful summer heat. Spring planting is acceptable if your soil dries out early.

Depending on your expectations and the kind of grass you grow, you may feed from two to five times per year. See the chart on page 71 for guidelines, and follow the feeding program specified on your fertilizer package.

Lawns in this region don't usually require a lot of watering except in the middle of summer. Avoid watering at night to prevent disease problems. If drought-caused watering restrictions are expected, gradually taper off watering to help the grass adapt to the drier conditions. If you wait until your town forbids watering, the grass could die, but if you cut back slowly the lawn will brown off but the roots will survive.

Crabgrass is the worst weed in northeastern lawns, but dandelion, ground ivy, plantain, nutsedge, annual knotweed, and clover can also be problematic. Billbugs and sod webworm (lawn moths) can cause trouble, but the worst lawn pest in this area is white grubs. Leaf spot is often aggravated by the region's high humidity but doesn't usually cause much damage. Gray leaf spot, however, does harm perennial ryegrasses and is becoming more of a problem.

Southeast

The Southeast region stretches from Washington, D.C., south to Florida and west to Mississippi, Tennessee, and Kentucky.

The best lawn grasses for the Southeast vary with the climate. In the cooler parts of the South, such as Virginia and higher elevations of North Carolina, cool-season grasses such as Kentucky bluegrass, fescues, and ryegrasses are used. Farther south and along the coast, coarser-textured warm-season grasses dominate.

Bermudagrass predominates in the warmer parts of the Southeast; ryegrasses can be used to overseed for winter color. St. Augustinegrass performs well in coastal areas from parts of North Carolina south, and throughout Florida to New Orleans, tolerating shade and salt. Centipedegrass is also used along the coast and tolerates acid soils. Both of these tolerate moist to wet conditions. Bahiagrass tolerates drought and sandy soil. Zoysiagrass is also used in the Southeast.

Plant warm-season grasses by dormant sprigs in March, or by sprigs or plugs from spring to midsummer. Plant cool-season grasses in late summer to early fall.

Because of the longer growing season, you may need to fertilize more often than is necessary in the Northeast. Consult the chart on page 71, and follow the feeding program outlined on your fertilizer package.

Watering needs vary with the amount of rainfall received and the type of grass in the lawn. Generally, Bahiagrass and Bermudagrass tolerate drier conditions, whereas St. Augustinegrass, and carpetgrass can take the most moisture. Other grasses fall somewhere in between.

Some of the most common pests in this region are southern chinch bugs, spittlebugs, grass scales, and Bermudagrass mites, all of which live on the foliage and suck plant juices. Sod

THE SOUTHEAST AT A GLANCE

CLIMATE: Mild; hot, humid summers; short, mild winters. Most areas get at least some frost; south Florida and the Gulf Coast are warmest.
SOILS: Vary from acid to alkaline; soils along the coast are poor and sandy; farther inland are clays, clay loams, sandy loams, and silt loams.
MOISTURE: Varies, with abundant rainfall in some areas and inconsistent rainfall in other areas, particularly higher elevations. Humid year-round but especially in summer.

Lawns in the Southeast are made from warm-season grasses (such as St. Augustinegrass, above) that tolerate heat and can be overseeded for winter color.

webworms, grass loopers, and armyworms eat grass leaves. Mole crickets, white grubs, and billbugs live in the soil and damage grass roots.

Mosses and algae can present problems in southern lawns, especially in shady areas where the turf is thin. The best way to remove moss and algae permanently is to improve growing conditions for the turfgrass by choosing shade-tolerant varieties; watering, fertilizing, and amending soil as needed; loosening compacted soils; improving drainage; and pruning nearby vegetation to improve circulation. To control moss right away, use a combination moss control and fertilizer, such as Scotts® Turf Builder® Plus Moss Control.

Thatch can also be problematic in the Southeast; dethatch when needed.

In winter, fertilize warm-season lawns overseeded with ryegrass. Mow cool-season lawns as recommended in the table on page 77.

THE NORTH-CENTRAL REGION AT A GLANCE

CLIMATE: Climate varies widely with latitude, depending on how much air travels north from the Gulf of Mexico and south from the Arctic. Summers are warm in most places, though cooler in the north, and winters are very cold in the northernmost parts of the region. Spring brings intense storms and the chance of tornadoes to the plains.
SOILS: Soils too are varied. Much of the region has fertile loess (wind-deposited soil), but prairie soils in the western part of the region are thin. Much of the region has alkaline pH, but parts of Michigan have acid peat soil.
MOISTURE: Moisture varies a great deal. The Great Plains are drier, getting most of their rain in spring and early summer, whereas areas south and east of the Great Lakes are wetter.

The best turfgrasses for lawns in the north-central region differ depending on local climates, which in turn vary with latitude.

North Central

The north-central region runs from Ohio west to Kansas and Nebraska, north to Minnesota and North Dakota, and south to the southern borders of Illinois and Indiana.

It's impossible to recommend one grass as the best for all of this varied region. The most commonly used turfgrasses in the Midwest are Kentucky bluegrass, perennial ryegrass, tall fescue, fine fescue, creeping bentgrass, and, in the more southerly, warmer parts of the region, zoysiagrass. Buffalograss is used in the drier parts of the plains. To find out the best grasses for your area, consult your local cooperative extension office or local garden center.

Plant cool-season grasses in fall, as soon as the hottest weather is past. Early fall is a good time to seed a lawn across much of the region for several reasons: The seed germinates faster in the still-warm soil; the cooler temperatures are favorable for cool-season grasses; there is less danger of heavy rains that could wash away seed; and there are fewer weed problems. You can also dormant-seed in late fall for grass to germinate early the next spring (this works best on level ground). Seed perennial ryegrass in spring, and plant warm-season grasses from late spring to early summer.

Mowing heights vary with the type of grass. See page 77 for recommended mowing heights. If long periods of wet weather keep you from mowing and the grass grows tall, when you are able to mow set the mower to the highest setting. When the clippings have dried, mow again to the desired height. If winter lawn diseases are problems in your area, make your last mowing in fall closer than normal, perhaps to 2 inches instead of 2½ inches.

During the driest part of summer, water once a week to provide 1 inch of water, so the soil is moist 6 to 8 inches deep.

Consult the feeding chart on page 71 and fertilize according to a regular program outlined on your fertilizer label; your local garden center can help you choose one that's right for your lawn conditions.

Remove thatch while the grass is growing actively so the grass can better recover from any injury it suffers. Dethatch cool-season grasses in early spring before the lawn turns green or in fall after Labor Day.

Other problems in this region include white grubs and Japanese beetles. The worst weed problems in this region are probably crabgrass and dandelions. Control crabrass with a preemergence herbicide applied with fertilizer in early spring. Control dandelions with a broadleaf weed killer applied with fertilizer in late spring.

Continue mowing until all the leaves are off the trees in fall. Avoid walking on the lawn when it has stopped growing, because it can't heal any injury that might occur. This is especially true for late fall mornings when there's frost on the lawn but the grass is still green.

Mow lawns to 2 inches high before winter.

South Central

The south-central region encompasses Kentucky and Tennessee in the east, stretching south to Louisiana and Texas and north through Arkansas, Oklahoma, and Missouri.

The best turfgrasses to grow vary with local conditions. Kentucky bluegrass predominates in Missouri. In warm areas Bermudagrass and zoysiagrass are grown for summer lawns. Buffalograss is useful for low-maintenance lawns in drier areas. Fine fescue and tall fescue are recommended for shade. Regional universities

recommend varieties that do well in their areas; visit their websites, or contact your local cooperative extension office or garden center for information on the best grasses for your location.

Fall is the best time to establish cool-season lawns; sow seed when the leaves have fallen from the trees. In spring, lay sod when trees have produced their new leaves. Plant warm-season lawns in late spring—May or June. Keep buffalograss free of weeds until it establishes; use a preemergence herbicide for annual weeds and a postemergence product for broad-leaved perennial weeds.

Fertilize cool-season grasses in midspring and again in early fall, or feed three times a year, in spring, late summer, and late fall. Fertilize warm-season grasses in spring and again in midsummer. Buffalograss needs little fertilizing.

Cool-season lawns go dormant in summer; if you water only during extended dry periods, the lawn will green up again in fall. To keep the grass green, water regularly, 1 to 1½ inches per

Lawn grasses recommended in the south-central region include Kentucky bluegrass, buffalograss, and other species in different parts of the region.

week, to keep the lawn from going dormant. Buffalograss needs water only during prolonged dry spells. Water deeply for all grasses.

Mowing heights vary according to grass type; see page 77. Mow cool-season grasses to 2½ to 3 inches in summer, no lower. Mow Bermudagrass to 2 inches or lower. Buffalograss can be mowed once or twice a month.

Dethatch if necessary when the lawn is growing actively. Pest and disease problems are most likely in the humid eastern parts of the region, particularly in summer. Watering in early morning and mowing high help prevent brown patch, pythium blight, and other diseases. Pests include chinch bugs, armyworms, and fire ants.

Northwest

The Northwest region includes northern California, Oregon, and Washington and runs east to Idaho, Montana, and Wyoming.

THE NORTHWEST AT A GLANCE

CLIMATE: The climate is quite varied, influenced by the Pacific Ocean and mountain ranges running north to south. Coastal areas are mild, with cool, often dry summers and mild, wet winters. East of the Cascades, winters are mild and summers are hot at low elevations; at higher elevations winters are quite cold.
SOILS: Soils range from sandy to clay, with high fertility in river valleys. Soils in rainy coastal areas tend to be acid; those east of the mountains are mostly alkaline.
MOISTURE: Coastal areas are moist and humid, with seasonal fog in some areas. Eastern parts of the region are much drier than western parts. Summers tend to be dry throughout the region, with much of the rain falling in winter.

Kentucky bluegrass and fescues grow well in moist coastal areas of the Northwest, but drier eastern areas need more drought-tolerant varieties.

The best grasses to grow in the Northwest differ widely across the region. Kentucky bluegrass and chewings and creeping red fescues grow well in many of the moister areas, with perennial ryegrass also included in the mix. A higher percentage of fescues is recommended in shady locations. Tall fescues are widely used in northern California. In drier eastern parts of the region, perennial ryegrass is often bypassed in favor of Canada bluegrass, sheep fescue, or turf-type tall fescues. For very dry conditions, wheatgrasses and bromegrasses are recommended, along with buffalograss and blue gramagrass. Consult your cooperative extension office or local garden center for information on the best turfgrasses for your area.

Seed cool-season lawns in mid-August to mid-September or, less desirably, in late April and May. Sow drought-tolerant grasses in fall. Lay sod in spring or fall for cool-season lawns, in spring for buffalograss lawns.

Fertilize new lawns at planting time. Follow a regular feeding program; see the chart on page 71 and consult your local garden center for recommendations best for your area and the grasses you are growing.

Keep newly planted lawns moist until seeds germinate or sod establishes new roots. Water established lawns when conditions dictate, but avoid frequent light waterings. Drought-tolerant lawns need occasional deep watering until they become established, but little thereafter.

Mowing height varies with grass type; see page 77 for recommended mowing heights. How often you need to mow depends on how quickly the grass grows. Mow higher during hot, dry weather and lower in cool, wet conditions. If necessary, dethatch before grass begins to grow in spring. Aerate, if necessary, in fall.

Moss is often troublesome in the Pacific Northwest. Control with a moss control and fertilizer, such as Scotts® Turf Builder® Plus Moss Control. Rust can be a serious disease problem in lawns that are underfertilized or watered incorrectly. Red thread can also strike if the lawn is underfertilized. Pests are usually not major problems for northwestern lawns, although crane flies can be troublesome at times.

Southwest

The Southwest region includes Southern California, Arizona, New Mexico, Nevada, Colorado, and Utah.

Recommended lawn grasses vary with latitude and elevation in this region. In cooler areas, Kentucky bluegrass is widely grown, and tall fescue and fine fescue are grown at low elevations. Bermudagrass can be used for warm-season lawns in the desert Southwest, and overseeded with perennial ryegrass in winter. St. Augustinegrass and zoysiagrass are also used in this region. In Colorado, drought-tolerant buffalograss, blue gramagrass, and fairway wheatgrass work as low-maintenance lawns in the high plains and mountain areas. Check with your local garden center for grasses recommended for your area.

Sow cool-season lawns in fall or early spring. Fall-planted lawns benefit from winter rains, but spring-planted lawns have a long, warm growing season to get established. Lawns from sod, sprigs, or plugs can be planted in spring or fall. Plant warm-season lawns in spring.

Overseed Bermudagrass and other warm-season lawns with perennial ryegrass in September.

Water is the big problem in the Southwest. Cool-season lawns need more water to maintain than warm-season lawns, although Bermudagrass also needs regular irrigation. Bluegrass and ryegrass may need more than 2 inches of water per week in hot, dry, sunny weather. You will probably need to water every two or three days. Water long enough to moisten the entire root zone if possible (use a soil probe or shovel to determine the rooting depth of your lawn). Watering before dawn minimizes evaporation. Some native grasses need far less water.

If water-resistant brown patches develop, poke holes in the soil with a screwdriver to allow water to penetrate.

Follow a regular feeding program; see the chart on page 71 and consult your local garden center for recommendations best for your area and the grasses you are growing.

Mowing heights vary with grass type. See page 77 for information. Weekly mowing is often necessary for cool-season lawns in spring, less often in hot, dry, or cold weather. Mowing to the recommended height helps prevent weed problems. Mow to the same height year-round.

Dethatch, if necessary, when the lawn is growing actively. Bermudagrass is especially prone to thatch.

Pests and diseases are less problematic in the dry Southwest than in wetter, more humid climates. Good cultural practices prevent most weed problems.

THE SOUTHWEST AT A GLANCE

CLIMATE: The climate varies greatly with elevation. Low-elevation areas are warm, with mild winters and long, hot summers; some areas are frost free. High elevations are much colder and depend on snow for much of their moisture. Coastal areas of California are subject to fogs and sea breezes, which moderate the climate.

SOILS: In much of the Southwest, soils are alkaline, sometimes intensely so, because low rainfall allows salts to build up in the soil. Some areas have an underlying layer of hard caliche.

MOISTURE: In inland areas, moisture generally increases with elevation. Rains are largely seasonal, and humidity is low. Evaporation and transpiration lose precious moisture. Coastal areas are more humid.

Turfgrasses recommended in the Southwest vary from Kentucky bluegrass in high-elevation locations to Bermudagrass and kikuyugrass in desert areas.

Grasses for All Conditions

You can grow a good-looking, trouble-free lawn in moderate shade if you choose the proper grass species and variety.

If your lawn seems to be struggling, you might be trying to grow the wrong grass. Maintaining a lawn is easy in good soil in the sun, but most of us are not so blessed. Fortunately, there are many turfgrass species that thrive in troublesome areas. Find the grass that best fits your site by matching your conditions to the appropriate columns in the chart below.

Shady

Many grasses tolerate some degree of shade, but the best also withstand high mowing, which makes more blade surface available for photosynthesis in low-light situations. If your lawn is shaded by trees, look for a good drought-tolerant grass because trees compete for soil moisture.

Dry

The best drought-tolerant grasses usually have long roots, which tap into all available soil moisture.

Hot

Heat tolerance is relative. Warm-season grasses can, of course, take the heat better than cool-season varieties. Some of them often jump the bluegrass line into the hottest areas of cooler climates. Some cool-season grasses, on the other hand, show moderate and even good heat tolerance and can be planted in cooler areas of the South.

Cold

Most cool-season grasses survive severe winters except those in the far North. Some, however, bounce back more quickly from the cold. Warm-season grasses vary widely in their ability to withstand cool temperatures even in the

HOW GRASSES MEASURE UP

Grasses	Establishment Speed	Heat Tolerance	Cold Tolerance	Drought Tolerance	Shade Tolerance	Turf Quality	Low Mowing	Fertilizer Needs
COOL-SEASON GRASSES								
Canada bluegrass	poor	poor	good	moderate	moderate	poor	poor	low
Creeping bentgrass	moderate	poor	good	poor	moderate	poor	good	high
Fine fescues	moderate	moderate	good	moderate	good	good	poor	moderate
Kentucky bluegrass	poor	moderate	good	moderate	moderate	good	moderate	moderate
Perennial ryegrass	good	moderate	moderate	moderate	moderate	good	moderate	moderate
Rough bluegrass	moderate	poor	good	poor	good	moderate	moderate	moderate
Tall fescues	good	good	moderate	good	moderate	good	poor	moderate
Wheatgrass	moderate	poor	good	good	moderate	moderate	poor	low
WARM-SEASON GRASSES								
Bahiagrass	moderate	good	poor	moderate	moderate	good	poor	low
Blue gramagrass	moderate	good	moderate	good	poor	poor	moderate	low
Buffalograss	moderate	good	good	good	poor	moderate	moderate	low
Carpetgrass	moderate	high	poor	moderate	poor	poor	good	low
Centipedegrass	moderate	good	poor	moderate	moderate	moderate	moderate	low
Hybrid Bermudagrass	good	good	moderate	good	poor	good	good	high
Seashore paspalum	moderate	good	poor	moderate	moderate	moderate	moderate	low
St. Augustinegrass	moderate	good	poor	moderate	good	good	poor	moderate
Zoysiagrass	poor	good	moderate	good	moderate	good	good	low

ADVANCES IN GRASSES

Turfgrass breeding made a remarkable leap in the second half of the 20th century. Before then, only a handful of commonly used turfgrass varieties existed, and most of them had serious shortcomings. They were often coarse texture and light color and had no resistance to insects or diseases. For the most part, they came straight from the pasture and had not been improved substantially for hundreds of years.

Things changed with dizzying speed. In 1960, there were six Kentucky bluegrass varieties. By the turn of the 21st century, there were more than 70. There was one perennial ryegrass variety in 1960. Now there are more than a hundred. In 1960 there were two pale and weedy-looking tall fescues. Now there are at least a hundred, and they look almost as good as Kentucky bluegrass.

With turfgrass breeding, grass blades have become finer and greener, and the plants are tougher and more dense. Perhaps most significantly, breeders have imbued grasses with resistance to virtually every lawn disease known. And now, thanks to endophytes—microscopic fungi bred into grass varieties— many grasses have resistance to insects as well.

Where do these new varieties come from? It starts with selection. Breeders scour the countryside for plants that exhibit outstanding characteristics: better color, vigor, and drought tolerance. Then they take them to trial grounds and test them. The grasses may be crossed with other improved plants to create hybrids, or simply grown out and reselected.

Research into improving turfgrass is ongoing. Scientists continue to search for ways to improve disease resistance, drought tolerance, and hardiness. To develop better disease resistance, researchers are studying various disease pathogens and how they work, and how weeds impede the growth of turfgrasses and weaken them. Researchers are investigating environmentally sound management practices that can minimize the effects of diseases. Studies of cold hardiness include analyzing how ice and snow affect various grass varieties and investigating ways to minimize damage caused to lawn grasses by prolonged cold. For example, one possible approach might be to use snow cover to maintain the lawn in a dormant state through the winter.

Trial varieties may take 10 to 15 years to reach the market. But as they gradually appear on garden-center shelves, they improve the appearance and performance of lawns across the country.

South. In some cases, cool-season grasses are substituted for warm-season grasses in the coolest areas of the warm-season zone.

Slopes

Grasses for lawns on slopes need to tolerate infrequent mowing (because it is difficult to mow on slopes), little (or even no) fertilization, and dry soil (because slopes dry out faster than flat ground).

Traffic

For heavily used areas, grasses should have good vigor and strong crowns that can produce blades even under constant traffic. Avoid grasses that require heavy fertilization and frequent mowing.

MIXES AND BLENDS

Most cool-season grasses are sold as mixtures (a combination of two or more species) or blends (a combination of two or more varieties of the same species). Here are some typical mixtures for various conditions.

GENERAL-PURPOSE LAWN IN FULL SUN: Kentucky bluegrass and red fescue, or Kentucky bluegrass and perennial ryegrass.
SHADE: Fine fescue and Kentucky bluegrass; or Kentucky bluegrass, red fescue, and perennial ryegrass.
COOL, MOIST CLIMATES: Fine fescue and 'Exeter' colonial bentgrass.
WEAR-TOLERANT TURF IN SUN OR LIGHT SHADE: Kentucky bluegrass, perennial ryegrass, and fine fescue.
TURF FOR HEAVILY USED AREAS: Kentucky bluegrass and turf-type tall fescue.
MOIST, SHADY LOCATIONS: Rough bluegrass, Kentucky bluegrass, fine fescue, and perennial ryegrass.
FOR A FAST-ESTABLISHING LAWN: Kentucky bluegrass and perennial ryegrass.
WARM, DRY CLIMATES: Buffalograss and blue gramagrass.
COOL, DRY CLIMATES: Wheatgrass and turf-type tall fescue.

NEW AND IMPROVED
Lawns

If you're just not happy with your lawn and the grass seems to struggle no matter what you do, you have to face the question: Can this lawn be saved, or is it time to start all over?

The best answer to that question lies with a thorough examination of your lawn. Start by looking closely at the individual grass plants. Are they a fine-bladed turfgrass with good green color and a generally healthy appearance? If so, the lawn is probably worth saving. However, if most of the grass is a coarse-bladed pasture grass, naturally pale green, or frequently marred by disease and insects, there's little you can do to make it look better. It might be best to start over.

Next, examine the overall lawn. Is the turf unattractive because it's a mishmash of unmatched grasses? If so, starting over is probably the way to go.

How about diseases? If you're constantly dealing with brown patches, circles of dying grass, and other symptoms of disease, the lawn has an underlying problem. First determine the problem, then either start over or overseed with a resistant grass, which will eventually become the dominant grass in the lawn.

REPLACE OR REPAIR?

It can be difficult to decide the best way to cure an ailing lawn and starting all over may be tempting. However, even if your lawn is troublesome, it may not require such a drastic step. Before you make the decision—to replace or repair—answer these questions.

REPLACE THE LAWN?
If you answer yes to any of these questions, consider replacing your lawn with better grass varieties.
- Are you trying to grow the wrong grass for your climate and lawn?
- Does your lawn regularly turn brown during the summer?
- Is your lawn the last one in the neighborhood to green up in spring or the first to turn brown in fall?
- Is the grass outpaced by weeds in spring?
- Do warm-season weeds such as crabgrass invade your lawn despite control measures?
- Is most of the turf coarse bladed and pale colored?
- Is your lawn a series of patches of three or more different colored and textured grasses?

- Do insects (other than grubs) leave large dying or dead patches in your lawn?
- Does water puddle all over the lawn after a rain, causing the grass to turn yellow and lose vigor? Or does the grass wilt and take on a grayish cast when it's not watered regularly?
- Is your lawn more than 15 years old? Has it not been updated over that period with newer, improved grass varieties?
- Does your lawn not meet your expectations even though you have followed a recommended annual lawn care program of three to five feedings per year?

Use the Gallery of Grasses (pages 20-37) to choose the right grass for your conditions. If your lawn has problems with insects, replant with improved insect-resistant varieties. If diseases occur throughout the lawn at least once annually, install a new lawn of disease-resistant grasses.

Severe and consistent weed infestations and diseases are signs of underlying problems, such as poor soil. If your lawn consists of more than 50 percent weeds, it's best to replace it.

Water puddling on the soil surface and wilting turf indicate that the soil needs improvement. To do that, you'll have to remove the turf.

After selecting the right grass and correcting underlying problems, follow the instructions on pages 52-61 for installing a new lawn.

REPAIR THE LAWN?
If you answer yes to most or all of these questions, a mere lawn repair is all you need.
- Most of the grass is fine bladed and deep green.
- The grass may be slightly thin but is generally healthy.
- The lawn is less than 50 percent weeds.
- Diseases occur only occasionally, if at all.
- Grass turns brown only during the most severe droughts.

Repairing your lawn may consist of increasing your fertilizing and watering regime, overseeding with new varieties, aerating, and top-dressing.

Is the sod thick or thin? You shouldn't be able to see bare ground between grass plants. And if the lawn is thin, chances are weeds have moved in to fill the available space.

If you can see bare soil but the plants seem healthy and are aesthetically pleasing, you may not need to start from scratch. Overseeding might be enough to thicken the lawn.

But if 50 percent or more of the lawn is bare, weed infested, or diseased, or has other problems, it's probably worthwhile to dig it up and replace it. If it's less than 50 percent problematic, you can get good results by merely repairing those areas.

Before either repairing or replacing the lawn, you must correct the underlying cause of the problems. Otherwise, the new grass will probably end up with the same problems. So the next step is to look for causes. One of the first places to check is the soil, which is often the source of lawn problems. Test its fertility, as explained on page 55, and look for thatch and/or compacted layers. If the soil needs extensive reworking, you'll have to remove the lawn to get to it, but first you might want to try aerating and fertilizing.

Another important step is determining whether the turf species in your lawn are the ones most likely to succeed (see Gallery of Grasses, pages 20–37). If not, you have one more reason to replace your lawn instead of repairing it.

Lawn that's less than 50 percent good grass (top): Start over. Thin, spotty turf that's in decent health (center): Rejuvenate. Thick, healthy grass with a few spots or weeds (bottom): Fine-tune maintenance.

Repair by Overseeding

If you'd like your lawn to be thicker, greener, more fine bladed, and more vigorous and stress tolerant, there's one relatively simple solution: Reseed it with a new, improved variety. At first thought, that may seem like an intimidating prospect, but it doesn't necessarily mean that you have to dig up and replace your old lawn with a new one.

There's an easier way: Overseed the existing lawn with new seed. You'll take advantage of the vigor and vitality of these new grasses. A variety that's well-adapted to your conditions will become established in your existing lawn and, in time, crowd out the older, weaker varieties.

Before overseeding, analyze the condition of your current lawn. If it has less than 50 percent good grass, your best choice is to remove the existing turf and start over. However, if more than 50 percent of the lawn is strong, vigorous grass, overseeding is a viable option. Next, try to determine what caused the deterioration of your existing turf. Was it shade? Drought? Insects or disease? Starvation?

Only after you've determined the cause can you choose appropriate new grass for overseeding. For example, select a shade-tolerant seed blend for shady lawns or a blend containing insect-resistant perennial ryegrass if insect infestations have ruined your cool-season lawn. In the case of recurring diseases, you may have to call in a professional to make a diagnosis, then choose a new seed blend resistant to disease.

You'll have better results if you do a little prep work first. Then be ready to do some follow-up care.

First, choose the best time for germination. That's fall for cool-season turfgrasses and spring for warm-season grasses. (For overseeding southern lawns for winter color, see box on page 49.) Then follow the steps for overseeding on page 49. Once the grasses are established, continue with your normal feeding, watering, and mowing regime; in time, the new grasses will take over the lawn.

If your lawn is thin but not too weedy and the existing grass is attractive and healthy, you may not need to start a new lawn from scratch. Rather than replacing the entire lawn, you can repair it by overseeding. The lawn shown below right has new life since it was reseeded with a new variety of grass right over the old, existing lawn.

OVERSEEDING STEP BY STEP

The success of overseeding depends how well the seeds make contact with the soil.

To ensure that the seeds are able to make contact with the soil, prepare the old lawn by mowing it as short as possible (A). Rake up the clippings, then mow and rake again. This helps expose the soil.

Next, scratch the soil vigorously with a metal garden rake to rough it up and create a good seedbed (B).

Because you're not sowing into bare ground, you'll need to sow seed (C) at two to three times the amount recommended on the package. Then cover the seed with a ¼- to ½-inch layer of topsoil, such as Scotts® Enriched LawnSoil®, or finely ground compost. Water daily until the seed germinates.

Mowing helps the new lawn fill in. Allow the new seedlings to grow to the maximum cutting height, then mow (D). You should take off no more than one-third of their height.

OVERSEEDING FOR WINTER COLOR

In the South, warm-season grasses go dormant early in winter, leaving a brown lawn the rest of the season. Because cool-season grasses thrive in the temperatures of a Southern winter, you can sow them over warm-season grasses to add some temporary color.

Choose a vigorous grass that germinates quickly in fall and dies back as the warm-season grass greens up in spring. If the cool-season grass grows too late in spring, it could compete with the warm-season species. Perennial ryegrass and red fescue are two popular species fitting these criteria.

Sow seed when temperatures begin to drop, usually in October or November. If you start too early, still-active warm-season grasses crowd out the cool-season grass. Start too late and the cold weather may inhibit germination.

The next spring, encourage the regrowth of the warm-season grass

by closely mowing the cool-season cover. The latter will die out as the temperatures rise.

Repair by Patching

To repair a spot, first square off the area by slicing through the turf with a spade, cutting 6 inches into good grass. Dispose of the sod.

Perhaps most of your lawn is in good condition with only a few troublesome spots, such as a weedy patch or a bare area. In this case, you don't need to replace or overseed the entire lawn. You can patch the problem area.

Correct the problem

Before doing anything, figure out what has led to the problem, especially if it's a chronic spot and not the result of a one-time accident, such as spilling hot charcoals on the grass. Unless you correct the underlying cause, you'll face the same symptoms again.

A number of possible reasons exist for bad patches in the lawn. Weedy turf could be due to soil compaction. Thin turf could result from shade, poor drainage, or lack of regular feeding. Heavy traffic or frequent use creates bare areas. A patch of yellow could result from gasoline, herbicide, or fertilizer spills, or from the family dog.

To reduce compaction, aerate the soil as described on page 86. Trim trees and shrubs to let in more light; if that's impractical, sow a shade-tolerant seed blend. (In large areas, it is easier to overseed than to make spot repairs.) For chemical spills, flush the soil well with water (see page 92).

Prepare the soil

Once you've corrected the problem, it's time to begin the repair process. The first step is to prepare a good seedbed for the grass (even if you will be just patching the area).

Completely remove whatever grass or weed cover exists in the problem area. Then square off the area to make patching more convenient. For best results, enlarge the area about 6 inches beyond the problem itself.

Next, prepare the soil as thoroughly as you would if you were planting a new lawn. Rototill it to a depth of 6 inches, removing any weed roots or rhizomes or any other debris, such as rocks or tree roots, in the soil. If the soil is sand or heavy clay, add several inches of Scotts® Enriched LawnSoil®, compost, or other organic matter and thoroughly mix it into the soil. Finally, rake the surface level, then water well.

Replant

BY SEED: If you're repairing the patch with seed, sow it at the recommended rate, then rake to cover with a thin layer

Next, prepare the soil as thoroughly as when starting a lawn. Remove debris, add organic matter and fertilizer, then smooth and level the soil with a rake.

Finally, patch the area by sowing seed. Use a grass species or variety that matches the existing lawn. That is, make sure it is similar in texture, color, and cultural requirements to the existing grass.

The fastest way to patch a lawn is with sod. Cut the sod to match the prepared area, then lay it so its edges touch those of the existing grass. Firm the sod into the soil.

of soil. In hot, dry weather, also cover the seed with a light layer of weed-free mulch. Or seed with Scotts® PatchMaster®. Keep the soil moist until the seed germinates. After the seed germinates, leave the grass unmown until it reaches its maximum recommended height.

BY SOD: Cut pieces of sod to match the area that you cut out and lay it as described on pages 60–61.

BY SPRIGS OR PLUGS: Some grasses are available as sprigs or plugs, which are ideal for repairing or patching lawns. Sprigs, also called stolons or runners, are small pieces of grass plants, complete with crowns and roots. Plugs are small, round patches of sod about 2 to 4 inches in diameter.

Generally, sprigs are planted 4 to 12 inches apart, depending on species, and plugs 6 to 12 inches apart. However, for patching, spacing

them closer together will allow them to fill in bare spots faster.

Before planting sprigs and plugs, prepare the soil as for sowing seed or sodding. Take extra care after planting. Keep the soil evenly moist (but not soaked through) for about a

month to allow the roots to become established. You must also be diligent about keeping the bare area between the sprigs or plugs weed free until the new grass has completely covered the bare ground.

To patch with plugs—small sections of sod— plant them 2 to 4 inches apart, making sure the roots are completely covered with soil.

For New Lawns, Start with a Weed-Free Site

Sometimes, after living with your lawn for several years, you decide changes need to be made. You might want to start a new lawn where one didn't exist before, perhaps to replace a garden bed. Or maybe you want to shrink the lawn to make space for more shrubs, or get rid of lawn grass in an area where it is not growing well.

If you want to start a new lawn, you first need to get rid of all vegetation growing where the lawn will be. There are a number of ways to eliminate weeds and old turf. Which method is best for you depends on the size of the area you need to clear, how much time and energy you are able to devote to the project, and how much money you want to spend.

If it's a small area and you have plenty of time and energy to spare, you can pull perennial weeds by hand. If you choose this method you will need to pull weeds every week throughout the growing season. Pull perennial weeds in such a way that you remove all of their roots, and remove all weeds before they set seed. Because weed seeds can remain viable in soil for many years and the tilling required for preparing a new lawn bed will bring many of those seeds to the surface, you will probably still need to control the sprouting of weeds with the application of preemergence herbicide each fall and spring. Be sure to wait at least six weeks after sowing grass seed before applying such herbicides.

Using herbicides

The easiest and most effective way to get rid of nongrassy weeds in an existing lawn before overseeding or patching is to use a selective herbicide that kills only broad-leaved weeds while leaving grass healthy and unaffected.

Nonselective herbicides such as Roundup® Weed & Grass Killer, or other weed killers containing glyphosate, kill all vegetation in the lawn, including grassy and broad-leaved weeds as well as existing turf grass. This is the easiest and quickest way to completely clear an area where you want to start a new lawn, or to get rid of lawn grass in places where you no longer want it.

Herbicides work quickly and require virtually no physical labor. There are some guidelines to observe, however, to optimize their effectiveness and safety. Always follow manufacturers' directions for application. Use only as much of the product as you need. Wear gloves and avoid inhaling the material. Take care to keep the spray off nearby plants that you want to keep. Avoid spraying herbicides on windy days, when fine sprays can drift long distances. Cover nearby plants with a tarp or use some other kind of physical barrier. Avoid spraying in very hot weather; some herbicides can volatilize and adversely affect the health of nearby plants.

Digging up sod

You can remove sod in small areas with a rented sod stripper or with a sharp spade. To remove sod with a spade, mark off the area you need to clear with stakes and string. Push the blade of the spade vertically into the turf

A sod stripper, which can be rented at many garden centers, peels off about 6 inches of sod. The machine has a blade that is inserted into the turf. You can then follow along, exerting little energy. Roll up the peeled-off sod every 10 to 20 feet. These machines work best on flat, even surfaces.

to outline a small patch. Then shove the spade horizontally under the grass and push upward on the handle to pull the sod away from the soil. Repeat until the area is clear.

If you're working in a small area, solarization is a good option. Cover your site with plastic and let the sun do the work. In a couple of months, weeds, as well as most soilborne diseases, will have baked out of your soil.

Solarizing

Solarizing is a good, low-tech way to remove turf. Solarizing uses the sun's heat to raise the temperature of the soil so much that existing grass or other vegetation is killed. Solarizing will also kill weed seeds in the top 6 to 12 inches of soil and will eliminate many soilborne pests and disease organisms.

The best time to solarize soil, especially in the North, is in midsummer, when the sun is at its strongest. If you want to kill grass, water it before beginning. If you want to remove weeds from bare soil, till the soil, rake it smooth, and water if it is dry.

Dig a trench several inches deep around the perimeter of the area you want to solarize. Cover the area with a sheet of clear plastic 1 to 4 mils thick, and press it down onto the grass or soil. Fill the trench with soil to hold the plastic in place. Remove the plastic after one to two months if there has been a reasonable amount of sunny weather. Pull or dig up the dead grass and compost or dispose of it.

Removing woody weeds

Removing woody, deep-rooted weeds is a challenge—but if you're starting a new lawn, it's a critical step. Poison ivy and oak, wild roses, oriental bittersweet, kudzu, wild blackberry, and broom are just a few thugs

you will not want to have in or around your lawn. There are two basic ways to get rid of them.

First, you can pull or dig the weeds. Cut back the tops close to the ground. Dig up the entire root mass, and retrieve any pieces that break off. Many of these plants can regrow from root crowns or small pieces of root left behind in the soil. Watch the area for the rest of the year, and dig or pull any new shoots that come up.

Alternatively, you can apply an herbicide formulated for killing poison ivy and brush. Various products with this designation are available; always read and follow package directions carefully. Repeated applications may be necessary if new shoots appear on treated plants.

If your woody weeds are well established, you could hire a landscaper or lawn-care service with stump-pulling equipment to pull them out by their roots.

Shading out the grass

One last option is to shade out turf and weeds. Spread numerous layers of newspapers a few layers deep over the area you want to

clear, and moisten the paper with water. Cover newspapers with a six-inch layer of shredded bark or other mulch, soil, or compost to hold them in place and completely shade out all vegetation underneath. The paper will eventually decompose into the soil, adding organic matter.

You can instead cover the area with black plastic or heavier material, such as pieces of old carpeting, but if they're not biodegradable, you'll have to remove and dispose of the cover when the grasses or weeds are dead.

An easy way to get rid of weeds is to cover them with several layers of newspapers, then top with mulch or soil. You won't have to remove the newspaper after the weeds are gone; it will decompose in a few months.

Know Your Soil

Starting a new lawn from scratch offers an ideal opportunity to improve the soil beneath it. Experts unanimously agree that homeowners should take some time to get to know their soil and improve it before doing anything else. Take advantage of this chance to get the soil right before putting in your new grass.

All about soil

Soil is critical to the development of the root system of your lawn; water and nutrients must travel through soil at the right pace to feed the roots. If water and nutrients travel too quickly, they drain out before the roots can take them in. If they travel too slowly, the roots can't get enough of them.

An ideal soil is made up of solid particles (about 50 percent), air (about 25 percent), and water (about 25 percent). The three types of mineral particles in soil are clay, sand, and silt (which is a mixture of the first two); the predominance of one of these will determine your soil's texture. Sand particles are large and porous; soils that have a high percentage of sand often drain too quickly. Clay particles are small and stick together; heavy clay soils drain slowly, delivering water and nutrients too slowly. Silt

Particles in sandy soil (below left) are far apart, allowing water and nutrients to pass through quickly. Clay soil (right) has tightly packed particles, which keep water and nutrients from passing through. Loam (center) is a mixture of the two, allowing proper drainage of water. It's the ideal type of soil for grass and other plants.

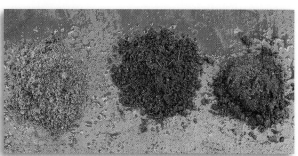

WHAT'S YOUR SOIL TEXTURE?

There are a couple of ways to get a rough idea of the texture of your soil. For the first test, take several teaspoon-size samples from the top 6 inches of the soil at several locations in your lawn. Let the samples dry thoroughly, then pulverize them with a rolling pin.

Fill a quart jar two-thirds full of water; stir in 1 teaspoon of dishwashing detergent, add the soil, cover, and shake vigorously. Over time the soil will separate into layers of sand, silt, and clay.

After about an hour, the sand particles will have settled to the bottom of the jar. With a grease pencil, mark its level on the side of the jar. After two hours, the silt will have settled into a layer on top of the sand. Mark the top of this layer. Finally, let the jar sit for two days; by that time, the clay should have settled out and the remaining water will be clear. Mark the top of the clay layer.

After you've made all the marks, you can estimate the relative amount of each kind of particle in your soil. If one type is more than one-half the total amount, that is your dominant soil texture.

The ribbon test is faster but not as precise. Moisten a handful of soil, then roll it between your open palms to form a ribbon or rope. If the soil feels gritty and doesn't hold a shape, it's mostly sand. If it feels smooth and silky and holds a rope or ribbon shape briefly before breaking up, it's high in silt. If it feels sticky and holds together in a ribbon or rope shape, it's mostly clay.

If your soil is high in silt or has equal amounts of each particle, just amend it as needed (after you test your soil as described at right). If your soil is high in clay or sand, amend it liberally with organic matter or compost (see list of amendments on page 56), or choose a grass type that works in the soil you have (see Grass for All Conditions, page 44).

All you need to test your soil's structure is a rolling pin, a jar, and a few teaspoons of dishwashing liquid.

falls somewhere in between. Good soil—sometimes called loam—has roughly equal amounts of clay, sand, and silt, along with organic matter (decomposed animal and vegetable material). If you are lucky enough to have loamy soil, you'll find that lawns—as well as most other plants—thrive. If your soil falls into one of the other categories,

SOIL ANALYSIS REPORT

Every soil test looks different, but here are some tips on how to interpret one.

PH: Lime is used to raise pH, sulfur to lower it. Changing pH is best done over a period of time.

PHOSPHORUS (P) AND POTASSIUM (K) are two of the main elements in fertilizer and critical to the health of your lawn. Nitrogen (N) is usually not measured because its level often changes as it leaches from soil or is used up by plants.

ORGANIC MATTER: The level of organic matter indicates the soil's fertility; if it isn't near optimum, add more (see page 56).

TRACE ELEMENTS: Micronutrients such as iron, calcium, and magnesium affect plant health.

APPLICATION RATE: A soil test report often advises how much of a corrective amendment should be used before planting.

SODIUM can reduce growth because it reduces the plant's ability to take in nitrogen.

WATER-HOLDING CAPACITY is usually a relative figure that changes with each testing service (sometimes nutrient-holding capacity is listed). If the number is low, discuss solutions with local experts.

	Result	Desired result	Recommended measures	Application rate
pH	6.4	6.5–7.0	Add lime	See below
P	18 ppm	20–30	Add fertilizer high in P	2 pounds per 1,000 sq. ft.
K	220 ppm	175–250 ppm		
Sodium	120 ppm	40–80 ppm	Discuss correction methods with agent	
Organic matter	3.2%	3–6%	Add organic matter	See below
Water-holding capacity	72	60–80		

Comments: Add 3 cubic yards per 1,000 feet of organic matter. Add sufficient lime to raise pH to 6.5.
Trace elements: Calcium slightly low; correct with lime.

you can improve it significantly, or you can choose a grass that will work well in your soil.

Soil testing

The first step in preparing to install a lawn is to have your soil tested. A soil test eliminates any guesswork about what amendments are required and gives you exact information about pH, nutrient deficiencies, and the presence of organic matter and harmful salts.

Many universities and county extension offices test soils for residents. Contact your local extension office for details. Private labs also do the tests; if none is listed in the phone book, call your extension office and ask for recommendations.

Some labs tell you only pH and the levels of nutrients major and micronutrients in the soil. Others supply instructions on how to interpret test results and what steps to take to improve the soil.

To get reliable test results, gather samples from several spots around the yard. Before sampling, scrape off the top 3 inches of soil from each spot. Take them with a core sampler.

Push this tubelike device into damp ground, then pull it out. It will extract a plug of soil about ¾ inch in diameter and 4 to 12 inches long. If you do not have a core sampler, use a clean trowel or shovel to take the samples.

Insert the sampler, then place the core in a clean bucket. Mix the samples together, then measure about a pint of this mixture and put it in the container provided by the soil lab. Label the container and mail it to the lab. If you have problem areas, sample them separately.

Amend Your Soil

Prepare the bare soil by removing all debris such as stones, twigs, and roots. Use a rake to level the soil and establish a rough grade.

While waiting for the results of your soil test, you can begin preparing the soil. First, remove all debris such as wood, stones, and large roots. Next, use a garden rake to establish a rough grade by filling in low spots and leveling hills. Measure the size of the lawn according to the instructions in the box on page 57. Once the soil test results arrive, you're ready to

Consult your soil test and apply the correct amount of fertilizer, then add organic matter. It's best to work amendments 4 to 6 inches into the soil. Do this by hand with a shovel in small areas. In large areas, a tiller works best.

After mixing in the amendments, do the final grade on the soil. When you're done, the soil should be level, with no high or low spots. You'll find using a long aluminum landscape rake will make the task go faster.

SOIL AMENDMENTS

Your soil analysis report will probably suggest some soil amendments commonly used in your region. Soil amendments are different from fertilizers. Fertilizers add nutrients to the soil; these fertilizers are consumed by the plants and often have to be replaced annually. Soil amendments change the soil's pH, improve its ability to hold and move water and nutrients, and help it to resist compaction. Some amendments are effective for only a year or two; others last for five years or more. Many soil amendments also add organic matter to the soil.

TO CHANGE PH: Most grasses do best in soil with a pH near neutral (from 6.8 to 7.2); there are a few that thrive in low pH (down to about 6.0) and high pH (up to 8.0) soils. Lime is the most common amendment added to raise pH; it is available in many forms that vary in causticity and speed of effectiveness. Sulfur, which also comes in several forms, is used to lower pH. Follow the recommendations in your soil analysis report for application rates.

TO IMPROVE DRAINAGE AND INCREASE WATER-HOLDING CAPACITY: Whether you have clay soil that drains too slowly or sandy soil that drains too quickly, organic matter is the answer. Two of the most easily used forms of organic matter are sphagnum peat moss and compost. Grass clippings and shredded leaves are also organic matter. Compost is decomposed plant material that you can purchase or make yourself. If you're not already making compost, ask at your local cooperative extension office for information on how to do it. Work organic matter into the soil before planting a lawn. In subsequent years you can top-dress with compost.

TO REDUCE SODIUM: Gypsum relieves compaction in clay soils that are high in sodium. Gypsum has the consistency of flour and is just as messy to work with—imagine wind blowing in your kitchen while you're measuring the ingredients for a cake. If possible, use gypsum on a day when the air is still.

TO IMPROVE POOR SOIL: If your soil is generally poor, incorporate richer topsoil into it, such as Scotts® Enriched LawnSoil®.

SOME AMENDMENTS NOT TO USE: Avoid adding sand to clay soil; it will make it even less porous. Also avoid adding sawdust or other wood products unless they are fully decomposed; as they decompose, they use the nitrogen that your lawn needs.

add soil amendments. Spread the amount of fertilizer and organic matter recommended in your soil test results, and work it into the soil to a depth of 4 to 8 inches. The easiest way to do this is with a rotary tiller. Avoid adding organic materials high in carbon—sawdust, wood chips, or straw. They will rob the nitrogen from the soil. If you have not tested your soil, use a special starter fertilizer, such as Scotts® Starter Fertilizer, according to directions.

After tilling, grade the soil, then firm it with a roller. Water the soil, then let it settle for about a week. Finally, smooth over any rough spots that develop and do the final grade, making sure the soil is level throughout the entire area.

APPLICATION RATES

Many lawns are deficient in organic matter. Too often, grass seed is sown in subsoil after the topsoil has been removed. Even when lawns have been started in good soil, the organic matter level decreases over the years. A lack of organic matter contributes to compaction, poor drainage, poor water-holding capacity, and, by extension, excessive dryness or wetness. On the other hand, soils with a high organic matter content increase fertilizer availability, and plants grown in them are often more resistant to diseases.

Topdressing with compost is an easy way to regularly replenish the organic matter in your soil. But for seriously deficient soils, you may want to work in more than the shallow layer that topdressing adds. (One cubic yard covers 162 square feet to a depth of 2 inches.)

Area in square feet	Cubic yards of organic matter to mix into the top 6 inches of soil to achieve 10, 15, 20, 25, or 30 percent organic matter. (One cubic yard = 27 cubic feet).				
	10%	15%	20%	25%	30%
300	0.6	0.8	1.1	1.4	1.7
500	0.9	1.4	1.9	2.3	2.8
1,000	1.9	2.8	3.7	4.6	5.6
3,000	5.6	8.3	11.1	13.9	16.7
5,000	9.3	13.9	18.5	23.1	27.8
10,000	8.5	27.8	37.0	46.3	55.6
20,000	37.0	55.6	74.1	92.6	111.1
40,000	74.1	111.1	148.1	185.2	222.2

LAWN MEASUREMENTS

You'll need to know the size of your lawn for many cultural practices, including watering and fertilizing. If the lawn is a square or rectangle, the measurement is straightforward; use standard geometric calculations. For other shapes, you'll have to use a bit more geometry.

SQUARE OR RECTANGLE
Area = L times W
L = Length, W = Width
Example:
A = 90 feet × 60 feet
A = 5,400 square feet

CIRCLE
Area = πr^2
$\pi = 3.14$, r^2 = radius squared
Example:
A = 3.14 × 20 feet × 20 feet
A = 1,256 square feet

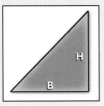

TRIANGLE
Area = 0.5 times B times H
B = Base, H = Height
Example:
A = 0.5 × 60 feet × 120 feet
A = 3,600 square feet

IRREGULAR SHAPES (accuracy within 5%)
Mark the length (L) of the area. Every 10 feet along the length line, measure the width (W) at right angles to the length line. Add these measurements and multiply the result by 10.
Example:
A = $W_1 + W_2 + W_3$, etc. × 10
A = 132 × 10
A = 1,320 square feet

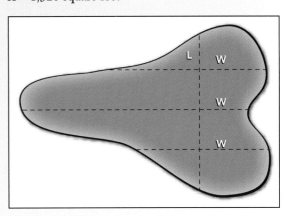

Start New Lawns from Seed

Just before you sow the lawn, use a metal garden rake to comb out any remaining rocks and make the surface as even as possible. Then roll it lightly with a lawn roller about half full of water.

Finally it's time to sow the seed. Calculate the amount you will need to cover the area you've prepared. (If you are planting an acre or more of lawn, you can seed in sections.) For large areas, use either a broadcast or drop spreader. In small areas, you can easily sow the seed by hand. Regardless of the seeding method, take care to get uniform coverage.

After seeding, ensure good contact between seed and soil by lightly raking the entire area. Avoid raking roughly. Doing so could redistribute the seed, ruin the final grade, and eventually bury the seed too deeply.

Mulch after seeding to keep the soil moist and hasten germination. You may use any number of materials: Scotts® Enriched LawnSoil®, finely shredded compost or dried manure, topsoil, or straw. Apply the mulch no more than ¼ inch thick and as evenly as possible. Then begin watering.

For seed to germinate consistently, the top layer of soil must stay constantly moist. Mulch will help but won't get you completely off the hook. You must thoroughly soak the soil to a 6-inch depth after sowing, then lightly water with a sprinkler as often as three or four times daily until the grass is established. Even a short dry period can kill the germinating seed. Use a fine spray or nozzle with a mist

Using the instructions on the seed package, determine the amount of seed required for the square footage of your lawn.

When using a drop spreader, ensure uniform coverage by slightly overlapping each pass.

setting to avoid washing away soil and seed.

Allow the young grass to reach its maximum recommended height before mowing (see the chart on page 77).

After sowing the seed, cover the area with a light layer of clean, weed-free mulch to keep the soil moist. Water it in well so the soil is wet to a depth of 4 to 6 inches.

GERMINATION TIMES

Grass species	Days to germinate
Bahiagrass	21–28
Creeping bentgrass	4–12
Common Bermudagrass	10–30
Blue gramagrass	15–30
Kentucky bluegrass	14–30
Buffalograss	14–30
Centipedegrass	14–30
Fine fescue	7–14
Tall fescue	7–12
Seashore paspalum	21–28
Perennial ryegrass	5–10
Wheatgrass	10–18

READING A SEED LABEL

Certain information must appear on all grass seed labels. Here's a sample label and what the terms mean.

PURE SEED PERCENTAGES
Percentages indicate the proportion of the grass by weight, not by seed count.

OTHER CROP SEED
This is seed of any commercially grown grass crop, such as timothy or orchardgrass. There should be minimal other crop seed in a good lawn mix.

INERT MATTER:
Inert matter includes chaff, dirt, and miscellaneous material that manages to escape cleaning. It should not exceed 4 percent.

WEED SEED
It is virtually impossible to keep all weed seeds out of a seed crop, but look for less than 1 percent.

TYPE OF GRASS
Look for quality turfgrass. Here, "Pure Premium" tells you that this is the best grass seed offered by this company, and is composed of improved grass varieties.

VARIETY
Named varieties are considered superior to common types and in most cases are a sign of a good mixture or blend.

SCOTTS® PURE PREMIUM™ SUN & SHADE® BRAND   GRASS SEED MIXTURE
NET WGT. 7 POUNDS

PURE SEED	VARIETY/KIND	GERMINATION	ORIGIN
34.33%	DIVINE PERENNIAL RYEGRASS	90%	WA
24.41%	ABBEY KENTUCKY BLUEGRASS	87%	OR
19.45%	FENWAY CREEPING RED FESCUE	87%	OR
19.15%	MAJESTY PERENNIAL RYEGRASS	90%	WA

OTHER INGREDIENTS
0.74%   OTHER CROP SEED
1.91%   INERT MATTER
0.01%   WEED SEED
NOXIOUS WEEDS: NONE FOUND

LOT NO: 13051
TESTED: JAN 2005 SELL BY: OCT 31, 2005
IN CO, IL, MT, NE, SD, & WI SELL BY: JAN 31, 2006
IN AR, AZ, CA, ID, NV, UT, OR, WA, & DC
SELL BY: APR 30, 2006
IN FL, SELL BY: JULY 31, 2005

THE SCOTTS COMPANY   AMS 661
144111 SCOTTSLAWN ROAD   1336S1
MARYSVILLE, OH 43041

NOXIOUS WEEDS
Some especially troublesome weeds, such as field bindweed, are declared noxious by most states. It is illegal to sell seed that contains these weeds. If present, they must be individually named and the number of seeds per ounce indicated. A good mixture will contain no noxious weeds.

GERMINATION PERCENTAGE
This represents the percentage of seed that germinates under ideal conditions. The percentage varies from species to species and can deteriorate over time. Avoid seed with less than 70% germination.

ORIGIN
When seed quantities account for more than 5 percent of the mixture, the label must show the state or country where the seed crop was grown; this will not affect how the grass will do in your yard.

TEST DATE
This is the guarantee that all the information listed on the label is correct. Buy seed that shows a date from the current year.

CARING FOR YOUR NEW LAWN

It takes up to two years for a new lawn to become fully established, with roots that can handle just about anything. Until that time, your new lawn—whether it's been started from seed, sod, sprigs, or plugs—is fragile. A little extra pampering will help it become established.

TRAFFIC: Keep off the grass for the first few weeks and avoid heavy traffic for the season.

WATERING: For the first 4 weeks, keep lawns that have been started from sod, sprigs, or plugs moist; water lightly but often (at least once a day; two or three times a day in very hot weather). Avoid soaking the soil under the grass; you want the roots to go deep to find water. For newly seeded lawns, water frequently but lightly until seeds germinate. If the seeds get too wet, they'll rot; if they dry out completely, they won't germinate and will die. After the first 6 weeks, water more deeply (until the top 4 to 6 inches of soil are moist).

MOWING: Avoid mowing until the lawn is at least 1½ times the high end of the height at which you will keep it. This might take a month or two. Mow on a dry day and make sure the mower blade is sharp so you don't snag and pull up the turf.

FERTILIZING: If you used starter fertilizer the day you seeded, you can wait to fertilize until 4 weeks after the day of planting. From then on, fertilize regularly, following the directions on the fertilizer bag.

PESTS, WEEDS, AND DISEASES: Check carefully once a week and treat any problems before they become serious. Discuss any problems with local experts and make sure herbicides you use are safe for young plants.

Start New Lawns with Sod, Sprigs, or Plugs

Sodding is the fastest way to a new lawn. Sod is grown on sod farms, such as the one above, then stripped off and replanted. If you decide to use sod, measure your lawn and prepare the soil before ordering. When the sod arrives, make sure it is green throughout, with no brown or dry patches. Each strip should also have a layer of soil and healthy white roots.

Seeding isn't the only way to start a lawn. The other options are sodding, sprigging, and plugging. You can sod a wide variety of cool- and warm-season turfgrasses; several warm-season grasses are available only as sprigs or plugs.

Sodding

Sod offers a number of advantages over seed. You can sod a lawn almost anytime during the growing season (you don't have to wait for the best season, as you do when sowing seed), and you can sod where seed may be hard to establish, such as in areas with heavy foot traffic or on sloping terrain. The most useful advantage to sodding the lawn is speed. A sod awn can be usable in as little as three weeks. Sodding doesn't mean you can skip any steps, however. You have to prepare the soil just as carefully as you would when sowing seed.

PREPARATION: Order sod about a week before the planting date. This allows the grower to schedule cutting or the local nursery time to order from its supplier. It's easy to estimate the amount of sod you need: Simply determine your lawn's square footage, then have the nursery or grower calculate the number of rolls you need. Buy that amount plus 5 to 10 percent more to ensure that you'll have enough.

If the soil is dry on the lawn site, wet it thoroughly a few days before the sod is delivered, then allow the soil surface to dry before laying the sod. Plan to lay the sod on the day it arrives; have the pallets stacked as close as possible to the planting area. If you can't plant the same day, put the sod in a cool, shaded area and keep the outer rolls moist. Lay the sod as soon as possible.

LAYING: The easiest way to begin laying sod is to start near a straight edge, such as a sidewalk or driveway. If you

As you lay the sod, make sure that the pieces butt up tightly against one another and all the roots are in firm contact with the soil.

If there are small, odd-shape, hard-to-fill patches, cut the sod with a sharp knife to fit those spots.

have an irregular shape lawn, create a straight line by drawing one on it with spray paint or lime or by stringing a line across it.

Handle the sod strips carefully to avoid tearing or stretching them. When rolling them out, stand or kneel on a piece of plywood to distribute your weight evenly. Unroll the first roll. Butt the end of the second one tightly against the first and unroll it carefully. Repeat this process until you have laid one complete strip across your lawn.

With each successive strip, tightly fit both the ends and the edges against one another. Stagger the ends, much as a bricklayer staggers bricks. After laying all the sod, roll a water-filled roller across it to ensure good contact between sod and soil.

After rolling the sod, apply a special starter fertilizer and water thoroughly. From then on, watch your new lawn closely. The edges of the sod strips will be the first places to dry out and may need daily watering. Make sure the underlying soil stays moist for at least the first two weeks.

Sprigging and plugging

Some warm-season grasses do not set viable seed and can be grown only vegetatively, such as by sprigs and plugs. Sprigs (also called stolons or runners) are pieces of torn-up sod of creeping grasses. Plugs are small squares or circles of sod. You plant each type at intervals, several inches apart, and eventually they grow together.

Sprig planting is best done from late spring to the middle of summer. There are several

Plant sprigs in late spring or midsummer. After preparing the soil, scatter the sprigs 4 to 12 inches apart and plant them 2 to 3 inches deep. Or plant them in individual holes or in 2-inch-deep furrows.

ways to plant sprigs. Dig 2- to 3-inch-deep furrows 4 to 12 inches apart, place the sprigs in the furrows, and firm the soil around each stem. Or lay sprigs on the soil at desired intervals and lightly press them in with a notched stick. The fastest planting method is broadcast sprigging. Strew sprigs over the soil by hand, then cover them with soil and roll lightly with a water-filled roller. Whichever method you use, apply a special starter fertilizer before watering them in.

Plugs should be planted in early spring. Before they arrive, use a steel plugger (or a trowel or small spade) to dig holes the proper size in the soil, spacing them 6 to 12 inches apart, depending on the size of the plugs and type of grass. To help the lawn take hold evenly, offset the rows of plugs in a checkerboard pattern.

When the plugs arrive, lightly moisten the soil and place the plugs in the holes.

Firm the soil around them so the crowns are level with the ground. After planting, roll as with sod and sprigs.

Water sprigs and plugs daily for the first two weeks after planting so they do not dry out. They may take up to two years to fill in completely, so it is important to keep the soil between them free of weeds until they have filled in.

Sprigs are pieces of grass stems.

Plugs are little pieces of sod.

To start a new lawn using plugs, prepare the soil thoroughly, then use a sod plugging tool or a small spade to dig holes 6 to 12 inches apart. Plant the plugs securely in the holes.

MAINTAINING
Your Lawn

What do you want from your lawn? Do you want coverage that stays green most of the summer, even if some of it consists of weeds? Do you want a neat, trim lawn with soft grass that's a pleasure to play on? Or is it a showcase lawn you desire?

It's up to you. When it comes to lawns, what you see is what you give—in terms of time, money, and dedication. There are innumerable levels of care for your lawn; here's an overview of the three most common regimes.

Low maintenance

With a low-maintenance lawn, you'll sacrifice appearance for the work you save. It will have its fair share of weeds. There will probably be some bare or thin patches of turf, and your grass may turn yellow or brown during dry weather. The lawn's overall appearance may be a bit shaggy. To keep a lawn from completely going downhill, you need to supply at least this much maintenance:

MOWING: At the very least, a lawn needs careful mowing on a regular basis at the prescribed height for the type of grass you're growing. Mow frequently enough so that the plant isn't shocked by losing too much leaf at one time.

WATERING: Where rainfall is sparse, deep watering may be required every week or two. However, in many regions, the lawn may not need additional water. Even if the weather turns dry, you can allow the lawn to go dormant.

FERTILIZING: A lawn needs some fertilization just to get by. Feeding at least twice each year—once in early fall and again in early spring—is highly recommended for basic health. Using a mulching mower helps too, as the grass clippings add nitrogen to the soil as they break down. Applying a preemergence herbicide as you feed the lawn in early spring will help discourage crabgrass.

Moderate maintenance

A lawn maintained at a moderate level needs more frequent care—you may spend twice as much time tending it. You'll still find weeds in this lawn, but they won't be as visible as they would with a low-maintenance regime. The grass should be thick and lush. Although your work and watering will prevent the lawn from browning out, it may not be bright green all season.

MOWING: Mow at least weekly at the top of the height range for the species. You may need to mow twice weekly during peak growth.

WATERING: Water enough to prevent dormancy from setting in. That may mean watering weekly during the hottest months.

FERTILIZING: Feed three times per year—in fall, early spring, and early to midsummer. Retaining grass clippings as mulch will improve nitrogen content.

WEEDING: Control weeds with herbicides or by pulling them by hand. In time, moderately maintained turf should crowd

out weeds. Aerate every two years or so to penetrate thatch and open up compacted soil.

Intensive maintenance

Consistent care is important if you want to have an award-winning lawn.

MOWING: Set the mower at the short end of the grass's height range. Mow frequently during peak growing season.

WATERING AND FERTILIZING: Provide 1 to 2 inches of water per week throughout the growing season. Feed at least four times per year: late summer to early fall, late fall, early spring, and early summer. In mild-climate regions with a long growing season, a fifth feeding is recommended in midsummer.

CONTROLLING PESTS: Following an annual lawn-care program that combines properly timed feeding with problem prevention and control is the easiest and most effective way to minimize problems with insects and disease (and weeds too).

No matter how you intend to maintain your lawn, the prescription is the same when starting from scratch: Improve the soil, organic matter content, and fertility to avoid problems, and use high-quality seed. Inexpensive seed results in nothing but headaches. Take time to shop around for quality seed with resistance to disease and the ability to stand up to the conditions prevalent in your yard. The result will be a weed-free bright green lawn.

LOW MAINTENANCE

- Mow regularly at the maximum height recommended for your grass species.
- Feed twice each year.
- Water only when grass is severely stressed by drought.

MODERATE MAINTENANCE

- Mow at least once a week.
- Water twice a month, depending on rainfall.
- Feed three times a year.
- Apply a preemergence herbicide when feeding in early spring; then apply a selective broadleaf herbicide when feeding in early summer.
- Aerate every two years.

INTENSIVE MAINTENANCE

- Mow weekly to semiweekly.
- Water regularly, depending on rainfall.
- Fertilize four to five times each year.
- Combine properly timed feedings with problem prevention and control for insects, disease, and weeds.
- Aerate annually.

Lawn Checkup

The first major step in launching a good lawn-care program is to take stock of the lawn's condition as well as that of its site. Check your lawn at least three times during the growing season: in spring and again in summer and fall.

Also, keep a journal for your lawn as you would for other plantings. Use the journal to keep track of lawn checkups and routine maintenance. Jot down when you feed, water, and mow, and note the lawn's response and any problems such as diseases and insects. Keep track of when they first appear, weather conditions at that time, and recent cultural activities.

Keep your lawn journal up to date. In time you will see patterns emerge, and you'll be able to prevent problems before they occur.

LAND: Start your checkup by mapping out the general lay of the land. Make note of slopes, wet spots, shady areas, and dead-air pockets caused by buildings and trees. Look for dry spots around driveways and sidewalks where snow, ice, or water accumulates during the winter.

GRASS: Then observe the condition of the grass, especially grass growing in heavy traffic areas. Is it vigorous or lagging? Is it rich green or yellowish brown? Does it have brown patches or other indications of disease?

How many different grass species or varieties are growing in your lawn? In the South, it's probably one, but in the North there could be several. They may be well integrated, but you may find patches of one growing where it has found its favorite site.

The box on page 44, along with the descriptions and photos in the Gallery of Grasses (pages 20–37), will help you determine which species are present. The gallery will also familiarize you with the cultural requirements of each grass you're growing. Grasses vary considerably in their need for water, fertilizer, mowing, and other cultural practices.

SOIL: Part of evaluating your lawn is testing the soil to find out its fertility. Order a kit from the local cooperative extension office or a private

GRASS DETECTIVE

From a distance, all grasses look almost the same, but upon close inspection many show different characteristics. Those differences can help you identify the grass, then pursue a cultural regime to suit it.

Note the color of the grass. Is it a deep, rich green or is it yellowish? Keep track of its active growth period. Does it grow most vigorously in cool or warm weather?

Is it a creeping grass or a bunchgrass? Dig up a plant and note how it spreads. Does it have rhizomes or stolons? Measure the width of the blades. Check to see whether they're smooth or sawlike.

Now take a closer look. Examine the various parts of the grass plant. Note the shape of the blade. Is the tip boat shaped or pointed? Take a close look at the sheath—the wrapping that encloses the stem. Note its color and whether it's split or smooth. Then find the ligule, the thin membrane or ring of hairs inside the leaf at the collar. Are the hairs long or short? Using all of these clues, refer to the diagrams and text in the Gallery of Grasses beginning on page 20 to make an identification.

For an excellent interactive tool for identifying lawn grasses, go to www.scotts.com and click on "What kind of grass do I have?"

If grubs have been a problem in the past, apply a season-long grub control such as Scotts® GrubEx® to protect your lawn.

Remove both ends from a 2-pound coffee can and jam it into the ground. Fill it with water, then see if any chinch bugs float to the top.

soil testing service. Follow the directions for taking the test on page 54; within a few weeks, the lab will send you a report that details the soil's nutrient levels and pH, along with recommended fixes.

Lawns growing in clay soils often need frequent aeration. In sandy soil, they need extra water.

WEEDS: Weeds are inevitable in any lawn. Up to a point, the damage threshold is determined by aesthetics. But if your lawn consists of more than 50 percent weeds, you're fighting a losing battle.

INSECTS: Insects can usually be managed fairly easily, but first you have to recognize the signs of their damage. Look for chewed blades, damaged crowns, patches of brown, and loose sod. To check for crown-dwelling pests, such as chinch bugs, cut both ends off a 2-pound coffee can and jam it a few inches into the soil.

Fill the can with water and watch for chinch bugs to float to the top. Refer to the section on insects (which begins on page 108) for more information on scouting for insect pests.

DISEASES: Check for symptoms of disease, such as brown circles, discolored blades, and grass dying in patches. Note how long it takes the damage to spread, whether it disappears on its own, and how quickly the grass recovers. Keep track of whether these symptoms occur in response to a climatic stress or a cultural practice.

USING A LAWN-CARE SERVICE

Some people find that maintaining their lawn is a deeply satisfying exercise. But if you find it just a pesky task, look for someone who is willing to take over for a reasonable fee. Whether you hire a teenage neighbor or a national company, you can take some steps to make the experience more valuable.

■ Ask for a regular schedule of mowing and pesticide application. Check the schedule against the recommendations in this book and with local experts. The mowing frequency should increase at times when grass is growing faster, and decrease in fall.

■ Find out whether your service has insurance; if not, make sure your homeowner's policy covers the type of work done.

■ Compare companies by finding out what type of fertilizer they use. Is it liquid or granular? What are the active ingredients, and are they safe around children and pets? Do they offer a satisfaction guarantee? Do they offer other services such as aeration or seeding? Are they licensed by your state?

■ Inquire as to what type of training, if any, the company conducts for its employees. Anybody can spread fertilizer on a lawn, but a trained lawn professional will be able to spot potential problems and recommend the right solutions.

■ Watch your lawn and report any problems, including weeds, pests and diseases (or their symptoms), bare spots, and early browning.

About Fertilizing

Like any other plant, turfgrass needs nutrients to survive. Because grasses compete with one another and with other plants, and because mowing removes a good portion of their photosynthesizing surface, they can become nutrient deficient.

Grass plants require 16 chemical elements essential for growth. Three—carbon, hydrogen, and oxygen—are readily available from air and water. The rest must come from soil or fertilizer.

Nitrogen, phosphorus, and potassium are known as primary nutrients because plants use them in the greatest quantities. Nitrogen is by far the most important element for a lawn. It promotes healthy growth and gives lawns a good green color. Because some forms of nitrogen leach from the soil and it is the element used in the largest amounts, most fertilizer recommendations for lawns are based on the amount of nitrogen to apply.

Turfgrass has less need for phosphorus than for nitrogen, but phosphorus is essential for healthy growth. It stimulates early formation and strong growth of roots. Your soil will usually need only small amounts of phosphorous for a healthy lawn, except in the case of planting grass seed, sod, sprigs, or plugs. When establishing new grass, a starter fertilizer with higher levels of phosphorus is beneficial.

Potassium strengthens lawn grasses, helping them to withstand foot traffic, resist diseases, and conserve water. Like nitrogen, potassium is leached out of the soil, but at a slower rate.

Most commercial lawn fertilizers—32-2-3 and 28-3-4, for example—are heavy on nitrogen and light on the other two elements. The numbers represent the percentage of nitrogen, phosphorus, and potassium, respectively, in a bag of fertilizer.

Turfgrasses require secondary nutrients—calcium, magnesium, and sulfur—in relatively high amounts, but not as much as the primary nutrients. These nutrients facilitate nitrogen uptake by the plant and increase root growth. If calcium is not present in adequate levels in the soil, add it with periodic applications of lime. Dolomitic limestone supplies magnesium as well as calcium. Most soils naturally contain sufficient sulfur but, if necessary, add it in the form of elemental sulfur or gypsum (calcium sulfate).

Even though plants use only tiny quantities of micronutrients, such as manganese, zinc, and boron, they are as essential for growth as primary and secondary nutrients. However, apply them only when a soil

GRASSCYCLING

If you bag and dispose of lawn clippings, you're throwing away a valuable resource. Grasscycling—leaving lawn clippings in place when you mow—returns nutrients to the soil. Researchers at the University of Connecticut Agricultural Station found that over a season, clippings from a 1,000-square-foot area contribute from ½ to 2 pounds of nitrogen, depending how much you fertilize.

Those clippings decompose faster than you might think, and they don't contribute to thatch buildup. Clippings begin to break down almost as soon as they hit the ground. Within a week, nitrogen released from them begins to show up in new growth.

Successful grasscycling requires proper mowing. Mow when the grass is dry, and follow the rule of one-third—remove only one-third of the height each time you mow. A mulching attachment on your mower (most mowers have them) cuts the clippings into small pieces, which decompose faster.

Of course, you may have reasons for collecting clippings, such as wanting the lawn to be extra neat for an event or a concern that the layer of clippings is too thick. If you pick up clippings, the best place to use them is in the garden as mulch (where kids won't track them into the house). Or add them to the compost pile.

Don't bag your clippings! You'll save time and landfill space, and they will nourish your lawn.

Rainfall and irrigation dissolve the nutrients in fertilizer and move them into the soil. Once there, soil microorganisms break them down into a form that's available to plants. Plants then take up the nutrients through their roots and translocate them through the plant's vascular system to the leaves (red lines). The plant uses these nutrients, along with energy from the sun, to create carbohydrates, which it stores in its roots, stolons, rhizomes, and crown (yellow lines). Liquid fertilizers work a little differently—when they're applied, plants absorb some of the nutrients directly through their leaves.

test indicates a deficiency. Micronutrients can be toxic to the plants even at low levels.

The exception to this is iron. Iron is useful in the South and West and is contained in quality fertilizers sold in those areas.

How much fertilizer?

Each grass has an optimum fertility range, as outlined in the Number of Feedings Needed on page 71. However, several factors come into play in terms of which nutrients and how frequently you will need to supply them.

For example, watering leaches nitrogen out of the soil and makes the lawn grow fast. So if you water, your lawn will need nitrogen. Sandy soils tend to be infertile, and they readily leach nutrients; clay is just the opposite. Lawns growing on sandy soil need more fertilizer than on clay.

How frequently you need to apply fertilizer depends on the type of grass growing in your yard, the type of soil, and the maintenance regime you have selected.

FERTILIZER WORK SHEET

It's easy to figure how much fertilizer to apply when you use a good brand of fertilizer and a spreader precalibrated to match that fertilizer brand: Simply apply the fertilizer at the spreader setting listed in the instructions on the bag.

If your spreader is not calibrated to your brand of fertilizer, you may need to convert the analysis found on fertilizer bags (see page 69) to pounds of nitrogen per 1,000 square feet. First, figure the pounds of nitrogen in a package by multiplying the package weight by the percentage of nitrogen. For example, a typical 15½-pound bag of 29-3-4 holds 4½ pounds of nitrogen (15½ × 29%). Divide that number by the number of 1,000-square-foot units the bag covers—5 for the 5,000 square-foot coverage of a 15½-pound bag—and you learn that 29-3-4 fertilizer supplies 9/10 pound of nitrogen per 1,000 square feet (4½ pounds ÷ 5).

Fertilizer Types

Shopping for fertilizers can be confusing. The elements in them, especially nitrogen, come in many forms, formulations, and brands. To help make your choice a little easier, here is a look at the general classes of lawn fertilizers.

Soluble synthetic fertilizers

The least expensive fertilizers are soluble synthetics. These concentrated fertilizers are produced from a chemical reaction that uses organic or inorganic raw materials. Included in this group of fertilizers are sulfate, ammonium nitrate, ammonium, and urea.

Soluble synthetics readily dissolve in water and so are often called quick-release fertilizers. Their advantages are speed and predictability. Grass quickly greens up after application. And because soluble synthetics don't depend on microbial action to release nutrients, they are effective when soil is cold.

Soluble synthetics have several disadvantages, however. Their effects are short lived, so you must apply them multiple times in a growing season. Grass grows rapidly after application, requiring frequent mowing, then goes through a slump as the fertilizer runs out. In rainy periods or in well-watered areas, the nitrogen can leach through the soil beyond the reach of roots. Also, the properties that allow soluble synthetics to dissolve in water also allow them to pull water out of plants, which can result in fertilizer burn.

Inorganic water-soluble fertilizer

Composted sewage sludge, an organic fertilizer

[Granular form of synthetic lawn fertilizer]

To minimize these problems, many manufacturers combine soluble synthetics with the next category of fertilizers: slow-release fertilizers.

Coated fertilizer

Slow-release fertilizers

Also called controlled-release and timed-release fertilizers, slow-release fertilizers provide nutrients at a predictable rate. They ensure uniform turf growth throughout the season. You can apply them heavily without fear of burning the lawn. However, they do not provide as quick a greenup and may be expensive to use.

One category of slow-release fertilizer has the nitrogen bound in a complex molecular compound. Until the compound breaks down, the nitrogen is unavailable to plants. Ureaformaldehyde (UF for short) is the most common in this group. Because UF is broken down by microbes, nutrients are available to plants only when the soil is warm enough for microbial activity.

Other slow-release fertilizers contain water-insoluble nitrogen. There are several types of water-insoluble nitrogen, including IBDU (isobutyline diurea) and methylene urea.

IBDU releases nutrients most efficiently when soil temperatures are above 75° F. It supplies nitrogen for about 60 days. Methylene urea releases nitrogen through bacterial activity and so is dependent on soil temperature and moisture. It can be formulated to last the entire growing season.

The last group of slow-release fertilizers is the coated fertilizers. With these, individual particles of quick-release nitrogen are covered with a material that lets out only small amounts of nutrients at a time, usually only when the fertilizer is wet.

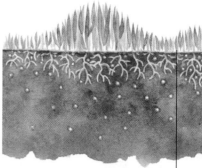

Surge growth: Fast-release fertilizers dissolve and move through soil quickly. Grass grows rapidly, then slows.

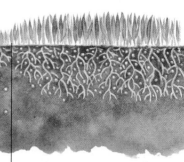

Steady: Slow-release fertilizers dissolve slowly. They spoon-feed nutrients, so the grass has steady, controlled growth.

By law, all fertilizer labels must include the same basic information.

The three large numbers are the chemical analysis of the fertilizer. They indicate the percentages of nitrogen, phosphorus, and potassium, in that order, making up the contents of the fertilizer package. In this product, the nutrients are combined in a ratio of 10 to 1 to 1.

Guaranteed analysis is the manufacturer's warranty that the stated analysis by weight is true.

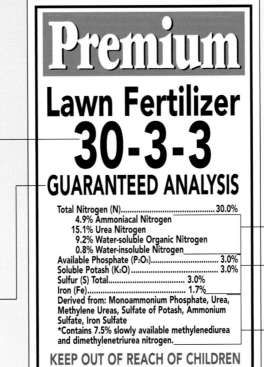

Premium Lawn Fertilizer 30-3-3

GUARANTEED ANALYSIS

Total Nitrogen (N)..30.0%
    4.9% Ammoniacal Nitrogen
    15.1% Urea Nitrogen
    9.2% Water-soluble Organic Nitrogen
    0.8% Water-insoluble Nitrogen
Available Phosphate (P_2O_5)..............................3.0%
Soluble Potash (K_2O)...3.0%
Sulfur (S) Total....................................3.0%
Iron (Fe)..1.7%
Derived from: Monoammonium Phosphate, Urea, Methylene Ureas, Sulfate of Potash, Ammonium Sulfate, Iron Sulfate
*Contains 7.5% slowly available methylenediurea and dimethylenetriurea nitrogen.

KEEP OUT OF REACH OF CHILDREN

Though not required by law, most manufacturers also list the various forms of nitrogen in the package, including the percentage of water-soluble and water-insoluble nitrogen. Because this product is mostly ammonium and urea, it is a fast-acting fertilizer. However, the addition of water-insoluble and water-soluble organic nitrogen means the product lasts longer than if it contained fast-release nitrogen alone.

All secondary and micronutrients in the fertilizer are also listed on the label by percentage.

The sources of the primary and secondary nutrients in the fertilizer package are listed after the guaranteed analysis.

Some manufacturers coat the particles with a semipermeable resin or plasticlike material and can formulate the fertilizer to release nutrients for a specified period lasting three to six months. Other coated fertilizers are a mix of pellets having coatings of varying thicknesses, which release the fertilizer at different rates. Sulfur-coated urea (also called SCU) is the most common of these.

Natural organic fertilizers

The term *natural organic* refers to any fertilizer that is made up of dried or composted plant or animal waste.

A wide variety of natural organic fertilizers is on the market. Among the ones most suitable for use on turf are those made from sewage sludge and poultry waste.

Organic fertilizers offer many benefits. Most have soil-building properties, improving soil structure and organic matter content in addition to providing nutrients. The nitrogen contained in natural organic fertilizers is usually water insoluble. Until soil microbes break them down, these fertilizers don't release their nitrogen. That means they release nutrients slowly, providing plants with a steady supply of food through the growing season. Thus, there's

little danger of overfertilizing with organic fertilizers or of excess nitrogen leaching through the soil. Organic fertilizers also often contain valuable micronutrients.

Compared with synthetic fertilizers, organics generally contain a lower percentage of nitrogen per pound, so you'll need to apply them in much greater amounts to achieve the effect that synthetic fertilizers provide. That increases the cost to fertilize. And because natural organics rely on soil microorganisms for the release of nutrients, they are weather dependent. They will work only if the soil temperature is above 50° F.

Blended fertilizer containing a mix of materials

When to Fertilize

"When should I fertilize the lawn?" It seems like a simple question, one that should warrant a straightforward answer, but nothing in lawn care evokes more confusion and disagreement than fertilizer schedules. Some say spring is the best time to fertilize; others recommend autumn. Some advocate both spring and fall feeding, whereas still others advise you to fertilize every month of the growing season. Who's right? All of them and none of them. In fact, there's no one right schedule. The time to fertilize depends on many factors, including where you live, the species of grass you grow, and the kind of lawn you want.

However, there is one general rule that nearly everyone can follow. It is best to fertilize your lawn when it begins its active growth period. This is usually (but not always) spring and fall for cool-season grasses. For warm-season grasses, it's late spring—after the grass breaks dormancy—through the summer. If you fertilize at the beginning of these periods, your lawn will have full benefit of the nutrients during the entire time it is growing.

However, there is one exception to this general rule. Late spring is not the best time to fertilize cool-season grasses with a quick-release fertilizer. At this time, quick-release fertilizer encourages lush growth, which may not be able to withstand summer heat. However, applying a slow-release fertilizer at this time helps the grass survive the stresses of summer.

Fall fertilization keeps cool-season grasses growing longer into cold weather, stimulating the lawn to thicken. As the grass slows its growth in fall, it stores carbohydrates to help it survive winter and get off to a fast start the next spring. Fall feeding provides the nutrients that cool-season grasses need to form the carbohydrates.

Warm-season grasses are a different story. Their growth peaks in midsummer, then tapers off in fall, continuing at a slower pace until frost. Late spring and summer are the best times for fertilizing warm-season turfgrasses. Make the initial application (using quick-acting forms of nitrogen) when the grass first starts to green up in spring.

Summer feeding keeps the lawn going through the hot season, but be careful about fertilizing in late summer or fall. That may promote a flush of succulent growth that leaves the grass more susceptible to injury when cold weather arrives.

How often you fertilize during these feeding periods depends on your choice of a maintenance regime. For low-maintenance lawns in the North, fertilize once in fall and again in early spring. In the South, fertilize once after spring greenup and again in early summer. For

SEASONAL FEEDING SCHEDULE

Early spring: Feed your lawn with a lawn fertilizer or with a fertilizer combined with weed prevention.

Late spring: Feed your lawn with a lawn fertilizer or with a fertilizer combined with weed control.

Summer: Feed your lawn with a lawn fertilizer or with a fertilizer combined with insect control.

Fall: Feed your lawn once or twice with a lawn fertilizer.

DIAGNOSING FERTILIZER PROBLEMS

Your lawn will show signs when fertilizer is not being applied adequately or correctly; sometimes, watching symptoms is more important than watching the calendar. Watch for these signs and react appropriately.

YELLOW COLOR, STUNTED GROWTH: Probably nitrogen deficiency. If adding nitrogen doesn't correct the problem, suspect an iron deficiency.
GRASS TURNS BRIGHT GREEN, THEN PURPLISH: Could be phosphorus deficiency, or just onset of cold weather.
YELLOW COLOR: Often means the lawn needs more iron or, rarely, magnesium.

SLOW GROWTH, REDDISH COLOR: This indicates a deficiency in calcium, which is rare and usually shows up only in acid soils.
STRIPED OR BLOTCHED PATTERNS IN GRASS: This sometimes occurs when fertilizer is not spread evenly.
BROWN AREAS: If not due to weather, this could be caused by burning caused by too much fertilizer.

Pale, stunted growth usually indicates that your lawn is deficient in nitrogen. Correct with regular applications of high-nitrogen fertilizer.

If nitrogen is sufficient and the lawn still won't turn a healthy green, it might be lacking adequate iron. Apply a fertilizer containing iron.

READ THE BAG

Most products used for lawn care—pesticides, fertilizers, lawn amendments—are safe, but only if they're used the way they were intended. Read the fine print carefully and pay attention to precautions. Ignoring them can harm your health and the environment as well as your lawn.

Whatever product you choose to fertilize your lawn, make sure you follow the manufacturer's directions for rates and methods of application. It may be tempting to put extra fertilizer on a struggling lawn. Don't. Grass plants can absorb only so much fertilizer. Follow the directions on the bag.

medium-maintenance cool-season lawns, fertilize three times: in late summer, fall, and early spring. Fertilize warm-season lawns in fall, early spring, and early to midsummer. For high-maintenance lawns, fertilize four to five times per year.

NUMBER OF FEEDINGS NEEDED

The numbers below represent the number of feedings needed, from minimum to maximum, for types of grasses used for lawn turf. Use the first number for a low-maintenance lawn and the higher number for a high-maintenance lawn. If your lawn contains a mixture of two or more grasses, use the average of their requirements. In areas with high rainfall, a long growing season, or sandy soil, adjust the requirements upward. Leaving grass clippings on the lawn may reduce slightly the amount of fertilizer required at each feeding.

Grass	Number of Feedings Per Year
COOL-SEASON GRASSES	
Annual ryegrass	3–5
Bentgrass	3–5
Canada bluegrass	2–3
Chewings fescue	2–3
Hard fescue	2–3
Kentucky bluegrass	3–5
Perennial ryegrass	3–5
Red fescue	2–3
Rough bluegrass	2–3
Sheep fescue	2–3
Tall fescue	2–4
Wheatgrass	1–3
WARM-SEASON GRASSES	
Bahiagrass	2–4
Bermudagrass	4–6
Blue gramagrass	1–2
Buffalograss	1–2
Carpetgrass	1–3
Centipedegrass	2
Seashore paspalum	2–4
St. Augustinegrass	4–5
Zoysiagrass	3–5

Fertilizing Techniques

Hand-held crank broadcast spreader

Drop spreader

Just as fertilizers come in different forms, so do their methods of application. Apply liquid fertilizers with a handheld hose-end sprayer. For dry fertilizers, use either a drop or a broadcast spreader, both of which you can purchase or rent from a nursery.

Always fill sprayers and spreaders over a sidewalk or driveway. If you happen to spill concentrated fertilizer on the lawn, hose it away or scrape or vacuum it up, then flood the area with water to avoid fertilizer burn.

HOSE-END SPRAYERS: This sprayer has a plastic or glass body suspended beneath a nozzle that attaches to a hose. Water flowing through the sprayer mixes with the concentrated liquid and propels it through the nozzle, spraying up to 15 gallons of fertilizer.

To use a hose-end sprayer, simply measure the fertilizer into the sprayer container and fill it with water to the proper level. Spray the entire contents of the sprayer onto your lawn, providing equal coverage to all sections.

The water and fertilizer mix together at a fixed rate. Always read the directions for both the sprayer and the fertilizer to determine how much fertilizer to measure into the container.

DROP SPREADERS: As the name implies, drop spreaders simply drop fertilizer from a bin. Their application is more precise than a broadcast spreader, but because they apply fertilizer to a narrower area, you have to make more passes. Drop spreaders are most useful on small- to medium-size lawns.

When using a drop spreader, overlap your passes enough so that no strips are left underfed, but also be careful not to double up on any sections. Missing sections will leave streaks in your lawn; doubling up can cause fertilizer burn.

BROADCAST SPREADERS: A broadcast spreader—either handheld or push wheel— is the easiest applicator to use for dry fertilizers. It throws the fertilizer granules or pellets over a wide area by means of a whirling wheel. The handheld model operates through a side-arm crank. It is best for small lawns. Not only is it somewhat awkward to use, but it is less accurate. The push-wheel model flings fertilizer from the bottom of a hopper as you push it across the lawn.

CALIBRATING A SPREADER

Most drop and broadcast spreaders have adjustable settings corresponding to the application rates on fertilizer bags. However, some fertilizer labels may not list your brand of spreader. Probably the easiest solution is to buy a new spreader with settings commonly found on fertilizer packages. Or you can calibrate the spreader yourself to ensure you apply fertilizer at the proper rate.

Here's how. If your spreader is equipped with a collection pan, measure its width, then attach it. Fill the spreader with fertilizer and operate it for a premeasured distance, say 100 feet. Weigh the amount of fertilizer in the pan. (If your spreader doesn't have a collection pan,

run it over a smooth surface such as plastic or a clean concrete floor, then sweep up the fertilizer and weigh it.) Multiply the width of the spreader by the distance traveled to determine the area covered. The fertilization rate of your spreader equals the number of pounds in the collection pan for the area covered.

For example, a spreader with a 2-foot-wide drop travels 100 feet and delivers 1 pound of material. The area covered is 200 square feet. Your spreader at this calibration applies fertilizer at a rate of 1 pound per 200 square feet, or 5 pounds per 1,000 square feet $(1,000 \div 200 = 5 \times 1 \text{ pound} = 5 \text{ pounds})$.

When applying fertilizer, a broadcast spreader is faster, but less precise, than a drop spreader. It throws fertilizer over a wider area but applies less fertilizer at the ends of its range. The best way to get uniform coverage with a broadcast spreader is to cover the ends of the lawn first, then go back and forth the long way. To avoid fertilizing an area more than once, shut off the spreader as you approach the end of a strip.

When using a drop spreader, it's best to go back and forth across the lawn. Overlap the wheel tracks enough so that no strips are left underfertilized, but also be careful not to double-feed any sections.

For either type, you need to know the width of the spreader's throw so you know how close to space your passes. You can easily determine throw width by filling the spreader with light-color material, then running it over dark-color pavement for a short distance. Usually, if you overlap passes by one-fourth their width, you can ensure uniform coverage and avoid streaks in the lawn.

The best technique for applying fertilizer with a broadcast spreader is to cover the ends of the lawn first, then go back and forth between the ends. To avoid double applications, shut off the spreader as you approach the end strips. Keep the spreader closed while turning, backing up, or stopping. For even, thorough coverage, walk at a normal speed and keep the spreader level.

Because it requires fewer passes to completely cover the lawn, a broadcast spreader is easier to use than a drop spreader, especially on large lawns. Streaking is also less likely with broadcast spreaders because the swaths of fertilizer overlap and the edges of the swaths are less distinct than those produced by drop spreaders.

Calibration

Both broadcast and drop spreaders have adjustable settings for use with different brands of fertilizer. Usually the spreaders come with a chart that tells you which setting to use for most brands of fertilizer, or the fertilizer has a chart on its bag. However, the openings in the spreader can wear out over time. It's a good idea to calibrate spreaders yearly to ensure that they dispense fertilizer at the correct rate.

One calibration technique is to draw a 100-square-foot area on a level section of concrete, such as a driveway or patio. Sweep the area clean, fill the hopper with fertilizer, then spread the fertilizer in the marked area.

Sweep up the fertilizer and weigh it. This tells you how much fertilizer the spreader is putting out per 100 square feet. To find how much it will apply over 1,000 square feet, multiply the weight of the swept-up fertilizer by 10.

Broadcast spreader

Benefits of Mowing

At some point, all of us have asked ourselves the question: What would happen if I didn't mow the lawn, if I just let it grow to its natural height? After all, it seems odd to spend so much effort and money getting the grass to grow, only to cut it back relentlessly.

The answer to the question is that the grass would grow to about 4 to 24 inches, depending on the species. As it grew, it would begin the natural process of sexual reproduction. The grass would produce flowers—no, not gorgeous blooms, not even attractive ones. The flowers of a grass plant are green, like the leaves, and grow on stiff, wiry stems. And they're a major source of allergy-producing pollen.

After flowering, the unmown plant would set seed, and the seeds would ripen and fall. Wind and foot traffic would bend over and break leaf blades and flower stems, making the lawn appear abandoned and neglected.

In the meantime, the turf would thin out because the outward spread of the grass is slowed by not being mowed. Mowing actually helps make the lawn grow thicker. You might say that because mown grass can't grow up, it grows out, but it's a bit more complicated than that.

The tip of each grass blade contains hormones that repress horizontal growth. Cutting off the tips with each mowing removes the hormones and allows the grass to spread outward more vigorously.

If you left the grass unmown, then later decided to mow it, you would cut off the plants' growing points. The result would be an even thinner lawn that's thatchy, because leaf and flower stems are what make up thatch.

All in all, if you let the lawn grow without mowing, using it

Maneuvering around trees consumes a lot of time while mowing the lawn. You can reduce the wasted time by surrounding trees with mulch to make mowing easier.

The more corners your lawn contains, the more time you'll spend mowing in and out of them. Design your lawn with soft, curving sides and no sharp edges and you'll save lots of time.

If your lawn does have corners, try this trick to save time. On your first mowing pass, round off the corners, leaving them unmown. After you've finished mowing the cornerless part of the lawn, go back and mow the corners. That way you have to deal with the corners only once, not on every pass around the lawn.

would be much less pleasant. Not only would the wiry flower stems make sitting and playing on the lawn uncomfortable, but also the thinning turf would not cushion falls as well and would be less safe for children playing on the lawn. Also, the long leaves would provide a good home for chiggers, ticks, fleas, snakes, and other possibly undesirable animals.

Mowing offers other benefits. It obviously makes the lawn look better, keeping it neat and trim all year. In spring, mowing removes damaged and brown tips. Mowing also helps deter weeds by keeping the turf thick with no holes for weeds to invade.

However, not every effect of mowing is positive. The very nature of mowing injures plants. The cut end is a site for pathogens to enter the grass plant. Every mowing is a bit of a shock to the plant, which forces it to put its energy into growing new leaves rather than roots. So the root systems of mown grass tend to be less extensive than those of unmown grass, and mown plants store fewer carbohydrates.

While trying to save time, avoid scrimping on mower coverage. When you mow, it's important to overlap each pass by at least 3 inches. That will ensure an even mowing with no skipped strips.

This dual nature of mowing has a big influence on how healthy a lawn is. Though mowing is, in a way, destructive, it is also positive if done correctly. And that's the key. Improper mowing is one of the most common causes of turf problems. The following pages will help you to do it right.

One of the best ways to cut your mowing time is to use the largest mower that's practical for your lawn. Mowing a one-acre lawn with a 24-inch-wide mower will save about an hour over mowing the same size lawn with an 18-inch mower.

Mowing Techniques

Every grass has a preferred mowing height (see box on page 77)—tall enough for the grass to readily recover from mowing and maintain a decent root system, yet short enough that the lawn doesn't become stemmy.

There's one other rule to follow, the rule of one-third. It says: Never remove more than a third of the grass blade at any one time. Suppose, for example, you have a bluegrass lawn, which does best with a 2-inch cut. To stay within the one-third rule, let it grow to 3 inches tall, then cut it back by 1 inch to restore the plant to the optimum height.

The importance of mowing height

Most plants have a fine balance between the size of their root systems and the extent of their shoots. When roots and shoots are in balance, plants are at their healthiest and able to survive all sorts of stresses.

Grass plants are in balance when you keep the lawn within the preferred mowing height range and don't cut off more than a third of the blade. When the blades are cut severely, root growth slows because energy is diverted to replacing lost blades. The grass plant taps into the carbohydrates it has stored in its roots and crown. These carbohydrates normally help lawns survive stressful periods of heat, cold, drought, and pest attacks. Without them, the grass might not survive the winter.

An occasional too-low mowing is usually only a temporary setback. But if you routinely scalp the lawn—cut off more than a third of the grass either by setting the mowing height too low or adhering to a rigid schedule—you can expect the lawn to become

A SCALPED LAWN VERSUS A CORRECTLY MOWN LAWN

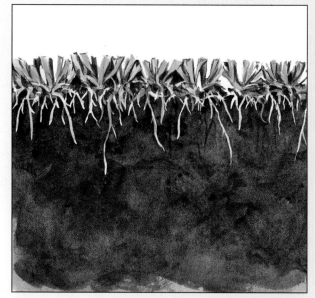

When grass is cut too short, or scalped, the growth of the roots is slowed and plant growth is virtually halted until the leaves can recover.

When grass is properly mown at its preferred height and with less than one-third of the blade removed, the roots continue growing and the grass thrives.

One of the most common and costly lawn-care mistakes is mowing the grass too short. Usually, lawns that are cut too short are scalped as well, losing more than a third of the blade each time.

Low mowing dramatically slows root growth. Scalping exposes brown grass stems. The grass is less healthy, and it looks it. A sure sign of scalping is a yellowish or brownish cast after mowing.

On the other hand, keeping the lawn within the preferred cutting height range and taking no more than a third of the blade allow the roots to continue growing deeply, which strengthens the plant.

less vigorous and more subject to stress over time. It will thin out, become weedy, and be subject to diseases and other problems.

If you return from vacation and are faced with an overgrown lawn, don't immediately try to mow it back to its preferred height. Instead, mow lightly, removing one-third of the blade or less. Allow the grass to recover for two or three days, then remove another one-third. Continue mowing until the grass reaches the right height.

Mowing tips

How and when you mow depend on several factors, including the type of grass, the season, and the amount of fertilizer and water applied. For example, you need to mow cool-season grasses more in spring and fall, warm-season grasses more in summer. The important element is flexibility. You may have to mow twice a week during peak growth periods or only twice a month during slow times.

Vary your mowing pattern. Always mowing in the same direction can compact the soil. Grass leans or grows in the direction it is mowed; altering directions will help keep it upright.

Avoid cutting wet grass. The cut will be uneven, and the clippings clog the mower as well as mat on the grass, blocking light.

For safety's sake, mow slopes on a diagonal.

If the ground is uneven, avoid scalping high spots by either raising the mowing height or regrading the area.

MOWING HEIGHTS IN INCHES

Grass	Minimum Height	Maximum Height
COOL-SEASON GRASSES		
Annual ryegrass	1½	2½
Bentgrass	½	¾
Canada bluegrass	3	4
Chewings fescue	1½	2½
Hard fescue	1½	2½
Kentucky bluegrass	1½	2½
Perennial ryegrass	1½	2½
Red fescue	1½	2½
Rough bluegrass	2	3
Sheep fescue	2	4
Tall fescue	2½	3
Wheatgrass	2	2½
WARM-SEASON GRASSES		
Bahiagrass	2	4
Hybrid Bermudagrass	½	2
Blue gramagrass	2	3
Buffalograss	2	3
Carpetgrass	1	2
Centipedegrass	1	3
Seashore paspalum	¾	2
St. Augustinegrass	2	4
Zoysiagrass	½	2

DEVELOPING A MOWING SCHEDULE FOR TURFGRASSES

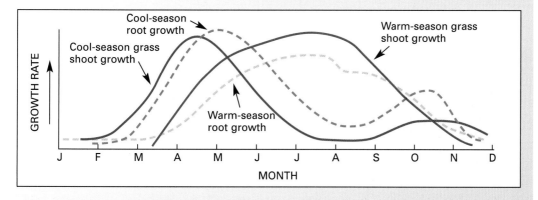

Rather than basing a mowing schedule on the calendar, decide when to mow based on the charts on this page. Here's how:

- Determine the maximum and minimum mowing height for your grass, using the chart above.
- As soon as the lawn greens up in spring, allow it to grow to its maximum mowing height, then cut it back to its minimum height, but do not remove more than one-third of its length at any one time.
- When summer arrives, allow the grass to exceed the maximum height by about one-third, then cut it back to its maximum height, again removing no more than one-third.
- Continue mowing at this height until fall, when the grass stops growing or goes dormant.

Choosing a Mower That's Right for You

We spend a bit of time behind our lawn mowers, but we don't know as much about them as we should. In fact, the mower we're steering across the lawn might not be the best one for the job.

There are two basic types of lawn mowers: rotary and reel. Each has its advantages and disadvantages.

Rotary mowers

Rotary mowers cut more quickly than reel mowers, are less difficult to adjust or sharpen, and do a better job of cutting tall, tough grass and weeds. Rotary mowers also usually offer a bigger selection of cutting heights than reel mowers, though most of them cannot cut lower than 1 inch.

All rotary mowers are power mowers. They may be hand-pushed (self-propelled) walk-behind mowers or riding mowers. Riding mowers have a much wider deck, up to 36 inches, compared to 18- to 22-inch widths for push or walk-behind mowers. With that width and their speed, riding mowers mow quickly and are recommended for lawns of an acre or more. Their size may make maneuverability on small lawns difficult, however, leaving lots of trimming to do by hand.

Many rotary mowers are engineered as mulching mowers. Specially designed blades and decks cut clippings into fine particles, which decompose rapidly. There are conversion blades on the market to turn your conventional mower into a mulching mower. However, mulching mowers are more than a blade. Baffles in the deck keep the clippings aloft until finely chopped. The conversion blade may not do as good a job.

If you choose not to mulch, or if grass is too high to use a mulching mower, many rotary mowers today have a mulch-or-bag option.

Reel mowers

Although they've been generally eclipsed by rotary mowers for the typical home lawn, reel mowers are still preferred for fine lawns. They conform better to land contours, and their scissoring action produces a cleaner cut. They are especially useful for lawns of bentgrass and Bermudagrass, because they can be adjusted to cut quite low. However, reel mowers are impractical for mowing rough, uneven ground or tall grasses with high, wiry seed heads.

You may recall heavy, bulky reel mowers. If you haven't used a new reel mower, you're in for a pleasant surprise. Made of durable lightweight materials, today's reel mowers weigh as little as 16 pounds, compared to 60 pounds for older reel mowers. Improved ball bearings, gears, and axles make them roll more easily. Height adjustment and blade adjustment have been simplified, and carbon steel blades hold an edge longer. The blades need sharpening only once every two years. You can take the mower to a shop for sharpening or do it yourself with a sharpening kit.

Reel mowers are available in several blade configurations, including four-, five-, and seven-blade designs. Seven-blade mowers are best for cutting low-growing, fine-

Rotary mowers have come a long way since their inception in the 1950s. Most of today's mowers are mulchers, equipped with blades that finely chop clippings and blow them down to the base of the grass plant.

Lightweight reel mowers are a good nonpolluting choice for small lawns. Look for mowers that allow you to adjust the mowing height without removing the wheels (inset).

If you have a large lawn, a riding mower is a good investment; they are expensive but save a great deal of time and energy.

Lawn mowers are fairly simple machines, but here are some extras that might make lawn care easier, more efficient, or faster.

- Aerators or dethatchers. Instead of buying separate tools, look for attachments that work with your mower.
- Robots. If you like high-tech gadgets, consider a robot mower. Just set it up and let it travel across the lawn while you watch.
- Electric startup. If you have trouble pulling the cord to start your mower, look for a mower that turns on with a key. Electric mowers have a long electric cord, so are useful only in small spaces.
- Mulchers. Most new mowers have a mulching attachment, which allows you to leave grass clippings on the lawn as mulch.

textured grasses such as Bermudagrass. Five-blade mowers are well-suited for other grasses; four-blade models are best for light use.

Riding mowers

Riding mowers are a great convenience, and there are many models on the market. You may not need all the bells and whistles that some models offer, but you will want good performance no matter what your price range. Here's what to look for in a riding mower.

You'll need adequate horsepower—15 or better for an average to large lawn, 11 for a smaller lawn.

A hydrostatic transmission is easier to operate than a standard transmission.

A rigid frame is stronger than a stamped-out steel frame. A cutting width (deck size) of at least 36 inches makes mowing go faster.

Safety features such as a weight-activated seat, which prevents the mower from starting unless enough weight is on the seat, are helpful for households with children.

Options such as cultivation tools and snowplows turn a riding mower into a multipurpose tractor.

Riding mowers are easy to operate, but it is important to follow all safety precautions when using one. Get some experience before you mow

on difficult terrain and avoid mowing after taking medication or when you'd be too tired to drive a car.

Buying a mower

It pays to buy the highest-quality mower you can afford. A good mower should provide you with years of reliable service. Look for equipment that is large enough and powerful enough for the job, especially if your lawn is big.

The money you save by buying a small, inexpensive machine may not be worth the extra time it takes to mow using inferior equipment. For example, cutting a 1-acre lawn using a walk-behind mower with an 18-inch cutting width takes at least 2½ hours. A riding mower with a 36-inch cutting width does the job in about 30 minutes.

Before buying a lawn mower, carefully look it over. Consider its maneuverability, starting system, and features for adjusting handle and cutting height. Make sure the grass catcher is easy to put on and take off and the safety shutoff handle fits your hand.

ELECTRONIC IGNITION

A mower with an electronic ignition is more efficient to operate than one with a standard ignition. Instead of points, it has a magnetic pickup, and there is no condenser. Fewer engine parts means the mower is easier to maintain and needs less frequent tuneups. The voltage is higher in an engine with an electronic ignition, which means a higher spark and a cleaner burn. A cleaner-burning engine has fewer emissions because it burns the fuel more completely. It is more efficient and thus emits fewer pollutants. Most lawn mowers have an electronic ignition; it's something worth looking for if you buy a used mower.

Lawn Mower Care

Keeping your lawn mower in good condition will extend its life and ensure that it will be ready to give your lawn a good, clean cut whenever you need it. Performing some regular maintenance procedures will keep your mower in tip-top shape.

The first step in mower maintenance is to read the owner's manual and become familiar with the maintenance routine recommended by the manufacturer. Here's a rundown of basic lawn mower care.

Routine maintenance

You will need to do some simple maintenance as you use your lawn mower over the course of the growing season.

First, always use fresh gas. It is best to buy just a gallon or two at a time instead of letting excess fuel sit in a 5-gallon can. Gasoline is best if it is used within 30 days of purchase.

Be sure to use the right kind of gas. Some older mowers have a two-cycle engine. (So do most string trimmers, leaf blowers, and some other kinds of small equipment.) Gasoline must be mixed with a small amount of oil to operate a two-cycle engine. For a four-cycle engine (which most new mowers have), use regular gasoline.

Second, keep the mower blade sharp to achieve a clean cut. If your mower blade has not been sharpened recently, examine the grass after you cut it. If the grass blades are left with ragged tips, the blade is dull. Make sure the mower is turned off and the spark plug disconnected. Then remove the blade. Sharpen the blade when the edges are no longer smooth and the surface is pitted. Treat any rust spots with a steel brush and steel wool. Then sharpen the edges with a grinding wheel or file. Some reel mowers come with a special sharpening kit. Or you can take the blade or the mower to a repair shop.

Finally, keep your lawn mower clean. Wipe or, if necessary, scrape off built-up grass clippings and dirt on a regular basis.

Annual maintenance

Give your lawn mower a complete service once a year, either before you store it for the winter, before the first mowing in spring, or at another time when your lawn is not growing rapidly.

Clean the outside of the mower thoroughly. Scrub off any accumulated dirt, grease, or clippings.

If you will be storing the mower, drain the gasoline or at least add a gas stabilizer to the tank. Change the oil too, draining the old oil and

SPECIAL EFFECTS

If you have a flair for the dramatic (and time on your hands), you could create patterns more elaborate than stripes. Maybe you'd like to make a diamond or lattice design or carve your house number or your initials into the lawn. After you lay out the pattern, the basic technique is the same as for making stripes. Adjacent parts of the pattern are mowed in different directions. These more fanciful effects are best done only for special occasions. Maintaining them would be more work than most of us have time for.

KEEPING AN EDGE

To cut cleanly, rotary mower blades should be sharpened about once a month under normal usage. Here's how to do it yourself.

First, remove the spark plug wire to prevent the mower from starting accidentally. Take off the blade by removing the nut that secures it to the mower deck. (You may have to wedge a piece of lumber between the blade and the deck to keep the blade from turning.)

Sharpen the edge of the blade using a file or a grindstone, following the angle of the edge. Take care to even out rough spots.

For a mower to run smoothly, the blade must be balanced. To check for balance, support the blade under its center.

replacing it with fresh. Recycle the old oil in accordance with municipal policy.

Check the engine and replace any parts that are showing wear. Examine the air filter and, if your mower has one, the oil filter, and clean or replace them. It's also best to replace the spark plugs annually. Lubricate the moving parts—fittings, cables, linkages, joints, and drive belts.

Tighten any loose nuts and screws you find, and any loose belts.

Make sure the battery is fully charged. If you find corrosion on the terminals, clean them by pouring a solution of baking soda and water over them. Then take the terminals apart and clean them with sandpaper.

FINISHING TOUCHES

Edging and trimming aren't necessary tasks, but they add a finished look to the lawn. Keep lawn edges sharp and clean with either a hand or power edging tool.

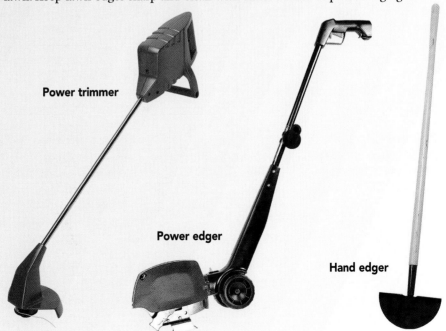

Power trimmer

Power edger

Hand edger

Watering Techniques

No matter where you live or what type of grass you grow, at some point you'll have to water the lawn. Exactly when and how often depends on several factors: the grass species, the soil type, the local climate, and the pattern of watering you have established.

The water requirements for a given lawn can range from a minimum of ¹⁄₁₀ inch per day in a cool or shady

Lawns need up to an inch of water per week in order to thrive. If nature doesn't provide it, you'll have to step in and water. You must choose the sprinkler carefully, though, considering flow rate, throw radius, and uniformity of coverage.

WATER NEEDS OF GRASSES

Grass species vary considerably in the amount of moisture they require and, conversely, in how well they are able to grow in wet or dry soils. Here are the general water needs of the major turfgrass species.

DROUGHT-TOLERANT GRASSES
Cool Season
- Tall fescue
- Red fescue
- Some Kentucky bluegrasses
- Sheep fescue
- Hard fescue

Warm Season
- Buffalograss
- Blue gramagrass
- Common Bermudagrass
- Hybrid Bermudagrass
- Zoysiagrass

GRASSES THAT REQUIRE REGULAR WATERING
Cool Season
- Creeping bentgrass
- Colonial bentgrass

Warm Season
- St. Augustinegrass
- Carpetgrass

GRASSES TOLERANT OF WET SOILS
Cool Season
- Rough bluegrass
- Canada bluegrass

Warm Season
- St. Augustinegrass
- Carpetgrass

location to ½ inch per day in full sun, hot temperatures, high winds, and low humidity. But that does not mean you have to water every day.

The soil under the lawn has a lot to do with how often you need to water. Sandy soils do not hold water well, so a lawn grown on sand may have to be watered two to three times a week if it doesn't rain. However, clay retains water well, and a lawn on clay soil may require watering only once a week.

Water the lawn slowly and deeply, moistening soil to a depth of 6 to 12 inches, and as infrequently as possible. Running a sprinkler for a few minutes every evening is the worst way to water a lawn.

If your lawn shows footprints after you walk across it, it's showing a need for water.

Roots grow only where there is water, so if you consistently wet only the top few inches of soil, the roots do not venture deeper. Eventually, the limited depth of the root system forces you into watering more often. That means trouble, because frequent watering keeps the surface wet, which is ideal for disease development. If roots go deep into the soil, they can draw on a larger underground water supply and the lawn can go much longer between waterings.

How do you know when the lawn needs water? The grass blades roll up lengthwise to conserve moisture. At the same time, they lose their bright green color and the entire lawn may take on a grayish cast. Thirsty grass plants also lose their resiliency, so if you walk across a lawn in need of water, the grass will not spring back and your footprints will remain visible.

LIGHT WATERING PRODUCES SHALLOW ROOTS; HEAVY WATERING PRODUCES DEEP ROOTS

You may think you're doing your lawn a favor by sprinkling lightly every day or two, but you're not. Light watering wets only the top layer of soil. If it's done regularly, the grass roots become accustomed to finding water there and grow shallowly. In times of drought, the plant then can't access deeper water.

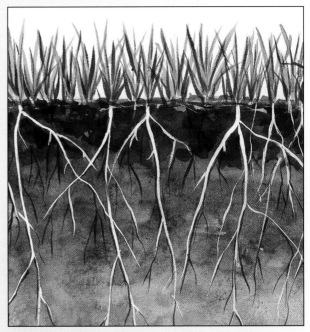

Correct watering—applying at least ½ inch of water twice a week—soaks the soil so that the water penetrates deeply. In this case, the roots don't stay near the surface; they extend deep into the soil, where they can gather water when the top of the soil dries out.

Sprinkler Varieties

There are several types of sprinklers, each with its own means of delivering water to your lawn and with its own strengths and weaknesses. When shopping for a sprinkler, you should consider several factors, including the size of your lawn, the type of soil, and how often you water. Match the characteristics of the sprinkler to your conditions and situation.

Choose a sprinkler that offers uniform coverage. If you have a large yard, you'll want a sprinkler with a long throw radius—the amount of ground the water spray covers—so you don't have to move the sprinkler too often. In general, a sprinkler with a slow flow rate is best because it prevents wasteful water runoff.

STATIONARY SPRINKLERS spray water in a fixed pattern through a small metal or plastic chamber pierced with holes. They are perhaps the least efficient sprinklers because their uniformity is poor and their throw radius is often short. Their flow rates may vary greatly. At the perimeter of the spray pattern, the grass may receive 8 inches an hour, whereas closer to the sprinkler it may get only 2 inches of water an hour. The area next to the sprinkler may stay dry. Stationary sprinklers are best for spot watering or to supplement other sprinklers.

OSCILLATING SPRINKLERS throw water through an arched, perforated pipe that sweeps back and forth, delivering the water in a rectangular pattern. In general, their throw radius and uniformity are good. Older models had the fault of depositing most of the water near the sprinkler head. Newer versions have solved this problem by stalling momentarily when the arm is farthest from the upright position, which allows more water to reach the outer boundaries. It's also easier to adjust the watering pattern on newer models, and some models let you change the width and breadth of the watering area.

REVOLVING SPRINKLERS shoot jets of water in a circular pattern from one or more rotating arms. Most models have a fair throw radius but relatively poor uniformity. More water falls on the outside edge of the circle, with most of the water falling between 4 and 8 feet out.

IMPULSE OR IMPACT SPRINKLERS rotate through the combined action of an internal jet and an external hammer, delivering pulses of water in an adjustable circular pattern. The head can be set to send out a strong jet, a gentle mist, or anything in between. This type of sprinkler is a good choice for large areas.

TRAVELING SPRINKLERS use the same mechanism as revolving sprinklers: spinning arms that shoot out water. However, as the name implies, the entire sprinkler housing travels over the lawn, following a path laid out by the hose. Consequently, they offer thorough coverage.

IN-GROUND SPRINKLER SYSTEMS offer convenience and efficiency. Revolving or fixed-type spray heads pop up when the sprinkler is activated, often by an automatic timer. The heads provide much more uniform coverage. The system must be designed so that the spray heads are installed at correct intervals to provide full coverage of the lawn. Because of this and the labor involved, it's best to have professionals install them.

ON AGAIN, OFF AGAIN WATERING

If water puddles up and runs off your lawn even after you've adjusted the water pressure, the flow rate of your sprinkler exceeds the ability of the soil to soak up water. Aside from buying a more efficient sprinkler, there is a technique you can use to solve this problem.

Rather than watering over one long period, cycle the watering. Run your sprinkler for 15 minutes, then leave it off for an hour to let the water soak in. Run the sprinkler for another 15-minute period, followed by another hour off. Repeat this procedure until you have run the sprinkler for a total of one hour.

SPRINKLER GLOSSARY

FLOW RATE: The amount of water delivered by a sprinkler per hour. In general, the lower the flow rate the better.

THROW RADIUS: The amount of area covered by a sprinkler.

PATTERN: The shape of the area watered by the sprinkler. You should match the pattern to the shape of your lawn to avoid over- or underwatering areas.

UNIFORMITY: A measure of how consistently water falls at various locations within the throw pattern.

Fixed sprinklers spray water from a series of pinholes in the sprinkler head. The water pattern may range from square to rectangular to circular or semicircular. In fact, some fixed sprinklers have adjustable heads to provide a number of different patterns.

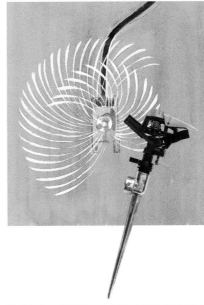

Impulse sprinklers shoot a stream of water from a jet nozzle, and the water is broken up into drops by a spring-loaded arm. These sprinklers usually throw water in a circular pattern. Most models may be adjusted to water only part of a circle.

Oscillating sprinklers shoot water from a slowly sweeping arm. Their normal pattern is rectangular, though most can be adjusted to throw water along a portion of the sweep. Because the spray shoots high into the air, wind easily deforms the water pattern.

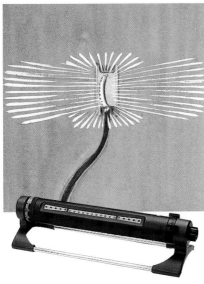

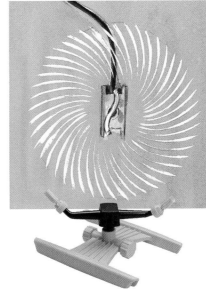

Revolving sprinklers shoot streams of water from a pair of spinning sprinkler nozzles. Because of this revolving motion, the pattern is always circular, and it is usually not adjustable. Also, more water falls on the outer edge of the circle than close to the sprinkler head.

Traveling sprinklers operate like revolving sprinklers, spraying water from spinning arms, but with one difference: The entire unit moves across the lawn. Consequently, the water falls in a series of connecting circles, so the amount applied is more uniform.

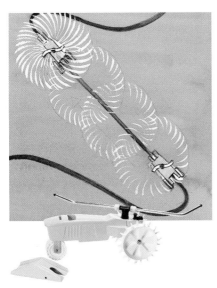

Pop-up heads are commonly used on small to medium lawns. You can select a variety of sprinkler heads for underground or in-ground systems. Heads are stationary or revolving and can be set to water quarter- to full-circle areas, or square or rectangular strips.

Aerating and Dethatching

Aside from the big three—fertilizing, mowing, and watering—you may need to perform two other chores, especially if you have your lawn on a medium- or high-maintenance program. These are aerating and dethatching.

Aerating

Many lawns, particularly heavily used ones, have compacted soil, which restricts the movement of air and water to roots. The soil under lawns tends to compact readily because, unlike garden soil, it is virtually never worked or turned. For the lawn, aerating is the alternative to tilling.

Intensively maintained lawns should be aerated once a year; those that receive moderate maintenance, every two years. Lawns with heavily compacted soil or severe thatch problems may need twice-yearly aeration.

Aerating is a simple process. It consists of perforating the soil (and any thatch above it) with small holes, which allow water, air, and fertilizer to get to roots. Aerating enables the roots to grow deeply and produces a more vigorous lawn.

Several types of tools are available for aerating lawns. If your lawn is small, there's a foot-press aerator that you push into the soil like a spade. For larger lawns, you can buy or rent an engine-powered aerator. This resembles a lawn mower, and you steer it across the lawn, aerating as you go.

Aerating tools remove thin, cigar-shape plugs of soil and deposit them on the surface of the lawn. Leave them there to dry for a day or so, then break them up with energetic raking to create a thin, beneficial topdressing. Make sure that the soil is moist, but not too wet, during aeration so the aerator can penetrate easily.

Dethatching

Thatch develops when dead organic matter—grass stems, dead roots, and debris but not clippings—builds up faster than it decomposes. It accumulates on top of the soil at the base of the blades.

The causes of thatch are numerous: poorly aerated soil, excess nitrogen, and too-high or too-infrequent mowing.

On a well-maintained lawn, thatch is rarely a problem. A thin layer (½ inch or less) is normal and does no harm.

The tight pores of compacted soil prevent root growth.

Compacted soil

Porous, uncompacted soil

No thatch

Thatch

Roots tend to knit into thatch, where they easily succumb to environmental stresses.

Power aerator

Foot aerator

Power thatcher

Cavex rake

Most of us tend our lawns according to a schedule that suits us. Usually that means doing yard work once a week whether the lawn needs it or not. We mow, fertilize, and water when we have a chance. However, our schedules may not always suit the needs of the lawn.

All lawns differ somewhat in the timing of certain tasks, but the following is a general guideline for chores you should be thinking about over the course of the season. The maintenance regime you follow—low, moderate, or high—will determine whether you actually do each task.

COOL-SEASON TURFGRASSES
Early spring:
- Examine lawns for signs of insects and diseases (see pages 108–121).
- Mow at the minimum height to enhance turf density. (See page 77 for proper mowing heights.) Mow whenever the grass height increases by one-third, perhaps as often as twice a week.
- Aerate if necessary.
- Establish new lawns or patch bare spots in existing lawns.
- Fertilize.
- Treat lawns with a preemergence herbicide for grassy weeds, such as crabgrass, if needed.

Late spring:
- Examine lawns for signs of disease and insects.
- Raise the mower deck and cut at the maximum height to enhance stress tolerance.
- Fertilize.
- Water deeply as necessary.
- If weeds are troublesome, use a grass catcher to collect clippings and weed seeds. Apply postemergence broadleaf herbicide if desired.
- Edge and trim as desired.

Summer:
- Treat for insect and disease problems if needed.
- Water deeply.
- Fertilize.
- Apply grub-prevention control.

Early autumn:
- If the thatch layer is deeper than ½ inch, dethatch.
- Fertilize.
- Sow new cool-season lawns or reseed bare patches in existing lawns. This is the best time for this task.

Late autumn:
- Continue mowing at the maximum height, taking off no more than a third at a time so the grass is well insulated in winter.
- For medium- or high-maintenance lawns, apply a fifth feeding.

WARM-SEASON TURFGRASSES
Early spring:
- Apply preemergence herbicide.
- Feed if grass has greened up.

Late spring, or as soon as grass has broken dormancy, greened up, and begun actively growing:
- Examine lawns for signs of disease and insects.
- Aerate and dethatch.
- Make the first mowing at the lowest recommended height to remove brown blade tips.
- Fertilize.
- Apply postemergence herbicide for broad-leaved weeds.

Summer:
- Examine lawns for signs of disease and insects.
- Raise the mower deck to the maximum height and mow often enough to remove only a third of the blade at a time.
- Fertilize.
- Establish new lawns or patch bare spots in existing lawns.
- Water deeply as necessary.

Autumn:
- Examine lawns for signs of disease and insects.
- Continue mowing as necessary, but delay mowing as growth slows so that grass goes into winter well insulated.
- Overseed with cool-season grasses for winter color.

In fact, it protects the crown and reduces soil compaction. A layer thicker than ½ inch prevents water from reaching the roots. If your lawn feels spongy when you walk on it, it has excessive thatch.

Because severe dethatching can weaken turf, it's better to deal with the problem before such action is necessary. The best time to dethatch is just before grass begins its most vigorous growth.

There are several ways to do it. For lawns with moderate thatch, simply aerating the lawn will do the trick. For small lawns, use a thatching or cavex rake to take up the thatch. The long, knifelike blades of these specialized rakes cut through the sod and pull up thatch.

For large lawns with serious thatch problems, the most effective tool is a vertical mower. Resembling a heavy-duty power mower, this machine has a series of revolving vertical knives that cut and pull through the thatch, bringing it to the surface. Rake up the material afterward.

Troubleshooting

If you're unhappy with the condition of your lawn, chances are that at least one of the big three lawn spoilers—weeds, insects, or diseases—is responsible. Turfgrass makes few demands, but when it encounters less than ideal conditions, such as shade, slopes, poor drainage, and poor care, problems quickly move in.

Your first instinct likely may be doing something to control the pests, and you can certainly do that. It's also important to recognize that weeds, insects, and diseases are often signs that something else is wrong: in your lawn, under it, or with its maintenance program. Rather than treating the symptoms with after-the-fact, quick-fix solutions, look at them as an opportunity to get at the cause of the problem. Sometimes a simple remedy, such as pruning overhanging branches that cause shade, will solve the problem without costing much time, money, or labor. In other cases, a laborious and expensive solution, such as reseeding the entire lawn or installing drainage tile, will be worthwhile in the long run. Remember, if you don't resolve the underlying cause, you will probably face the same problem in the future.

Before investing in any solution, consider the kind of care you're giving your lawn, the environment in which you want it to grow, the suitability of the grass for your climate, and its tolerance to common diseases and insects in your area. Here's a sampling of what can go wrong and some possible solutions.

POOR DRAINAGE: When water stands on the lawn or saturates the soil, grass struggles. Moisture-loving weeds, such as ground ivy and speedwell, move in, and pythium blight and other diseases thrive. If the problem is minor, simply aerating may solve it. But if drainage problems are serious and persistent, you may need to regrade the area or install drainage tiles to funnel water away.

POOR WATERING: Overwatering is as bad as poor drainage. Watering too frequently weakens plant roots, which provides an entrance for many diseases. Although underwatering can stress turf, most grasses will simply go dormant when water is scarce.

SLOPES: Soil drains irregularly on steep slopes. It may be too dry at the top and too wet at the bottom. Sloping turf is difficult to mow, fertilize, and water properly. That's why slopes often have more weeds than does level ground. If regrading is not an option,

HEALTHY LAWN REGIME

- Grow the proper grass for your climate and conditions.
- Test soil for nutrients and pH before planting a new lawn or if existing lawn does not respond to a properly timed annual feeding program. Correct as needed.
- Check soil for compaction at various locations throughout the yard.
- Aerate every year or two and top-dress afterward with topsoil (such as Scotts® Enriched LawnSoil®) or shredded compost.
- Check for thatch annually. Remove if it is more than ½ inch thick.
- Trim or remove trees and shrubs to reduce shade and increase airflow.
- Fertilize four to five times each year (see pages 70-71).
- Mow lightly and regularly. The grass should not exceed its maximum recommended height (page 77) by more than a third.
- Water infrequently but deeply. Run sprinklers twice a week long enough to put down ½ inch of water each time. Make sure the water soaks into the soil rather than runs off.
- Inspect the grass at least once a month: Get down on your hands and knees to look for insects, evidence of diseases, and weeds.

consider replacing the turf with a hardy groundcover such as crown vetch.

SHADE: Most turfgrasses are sun lovers. Shade slows their growth—blades become spindly and the turf thins out—and weeds and diseases get the upper hand. However, it's not impossible to grow grass in shade. Some species—most notably fine fescue, St. Augustinegrass, zoysiagrass, and some Kentucky bluegrass cultivars—are shade tolerant. If your lawn is thin because you've planted only sun-loving varieties in a shady spot, overseeding with a shade-tolerant mix might solve the problem without requiring a totally new lawn. Also, you can reduce the amount of shade by trimming trees; and by mowing higher and watering deeply, you can help the grass withstand the shade.

POOR MOWING: Mowing too low and too infrequently are common causes of disease and weed infestations because they weaken the grass. Also, the turf thins out under this kind of care, and any empty spot in the lawn is an open invitation to weeds. To forestall weed and disease invasion, follow the correct mowing schedule for your type of grass.

TRAFFIC: High-traffic areas—where you walk, play ball, or barbecue—are perfect spots for weeds. Many weeds are much better adapted than turfgrasses to the compacted soil that comes with heavy use. And as the turf thins under the traffic, the open spots offer places for weeds to move in. Consider planting a wear-resistant grass that won't thin out. Or replace the turf with hardscaping such as paving blocks or bricks.

Poor drainage

Poor mowing

Shade

Slope

Traffic

Poor watering

Site and Cultural Problems

Weeds, insects, and diseases are usually blamed for lawn problems. But several other common problems—some of them avoidable—might be the culprits. Chemical burns, pets using the lawn as a toilet, low spots with poor drainage, dry spots, scalping, root competition, summer heat and drought, and flooding all can take their toll on the lawn. Because of their symptoms, these environmental problems often are mistaken for insect or disease infestations. There are ways to deal with all of these problems. In the cases of heat and drought, you can be proactive. Take steps to prepare your lawn when you anticipate that these conditions will occur and you will minimize stress and damage to the turf.

The following descriptions and prescriptions will help you avoid confusion. Use these pages as a guide to diagnosing and dealing with issues caused by your site or the cultural methods that you practice.

LOW SPOTS WITH POOR DRAINAGE: If your lawn has depressions with pale, thinning, weedy turf where standing water gathers, you have a grading problem that must be corrected. If the low spot is not deep, you can fill it in gradually by spreading small amounts of soil (such as Scotts® Enriched LawnSoil®) over the low area and allowing the grass to grow up through it. If the

Dry spots

drainage problem is more widespread or severe, first try to alleviate it by deeply aerating the wet patch. This should allow water to penetrate farther into the soil. When the water has drained, roll back the sod, fill in beneath it with topsoil, and replace the turf.

DRY SPOTS: When grasses turn from bright to dull green and lose their luster in patches, the cause could be dry spots. These often result from compacted soil, fast-draining areas in an otherwise slow-draining lawn, or even buried construction debris. If the grass blades do not spring back after you walk across them, dryness is the problem. In lawns of cool-season grasses, raise the mower blade about ½ inch when you mow and make sure to

Poor drainage

irrigate those areas thoroughly. If compaction is causing the problem, aerate the soil. Check for buried construction debris by poking through the soil surface with a long screwdriver. If this is the problem, you'll need to dig out the debris, replace the cavity with good topsoil, and replant or patch the area.

SCALPING OR DULL MOWER INJURY: If the lawn turns brown soon after mowing, that means you've scalped it—removed too much of the grass blade at one time. The lawn will recover, but raise the cutting height and avoid mowing off more than one-third of the grass blade at a time. If the lawn turns grayish after mowing, the mower blades are dull. Again, the grass will recover, but be sure to sharpen the blades. Muffler burn can occur when you leave the mower running in one place for a while. The burn is ugly, but it will heal.

ROOT COMPETITION: Thinning grass that fails to grow vigorously and is paler than the surrounding lawn may be suffering from competition with tree roots. In this situation, it is usually best to plant a shade-tolerant grass seed blend or a ground cover. You can attempt to encourage the trees to develop deep roots that are less dependent on surface water and nutrients by watering deeply and fertilizing regularly. Many trees are naturally surface rooting, and the feeder roots of most trees occur in the top 12 inches of soil.

Dull mower blade

Muffler burn

Root competition

Chemical burns

eventually fill in. If the area doesn't fill in, replace the soil under the dead spots and patch them.

PET DAMAGE: When pets, especially dogs, do their business on the lawn, the grass can be damaged. Cats are generally less problematic because they deposit smaller amounts of urine and feces. Small amounts of pet wastes can actually make the lawn greener where they land because they contain nitrogen. But large amounts or repeated deposits on the same spot can cause burned brown patches in the grass. Often this kind of patch is surrounded by a green outer ring. Many of these brown patches will recover in time, but others will not.

You can try to prevent future damage in several ways. You might spray the area with a deer repellent or install a motion-activated sprinkler (although children could also inadvertently trigger the device). You could walk the dog so it doesn't have to use the yard. You might be able to train the dog to use another location by transporting its

CHEMICAL BURNS: Fertilizer or herbicides spilled on the lawn, gasoline leaking from the mower, or dogs doing their business: All leave distinct patches of dead grass, which are the hallmark of a chemical burn. In the case of fertilizer spills and dog urine, both of which contain an abundance of nitrogen, bright green grass will surround the dead patch.

There are a few ways to remedy chemical burns; you should act quickly and before symptoms appear. For water-soluble material, such as most herbicides, fertilizers, and urine, thoroughly drench the soil with water. For burns caused by insoluble material, such as gasoline or oil, first drench the soil with soapy water, then water thoroughly.

Once the symptoms appear, it is too late to save the browned grass. However, if the burned area is small, surrounding grass may

Core aeration removes many cigar-shape sections of stressed roots (left), allowing new, deep roots (right) to take their place. It relieves problems caused by flooding as well as normal compaction.

waste to the new area and rewarding the dog when it goes where you want it to. For this technique to work, you have to do it consistently for at least two weeks. You might also consult your veterinarian about possible dietary changes that might help.

Once the damage has been done, water the area thoroughly within eight hours to dilute the urine. Otherwise, let the grass regrow over time unless you think that weeds may colonize the site. In that case, dig up the damaged grass and sow fresh seed or resod the area.

MINIMIZING DAMAGE FROM HEAT AND DROUGHT: Hot or dry weather can wreak havoc on a lawn, but you can precondition yours to better withstand these stresses. A healthy lawn can better tolerate adverse weather, so follow the procedures recommended in this book to get your lawn in peak condition before the heat and drought set in.

In the early stages of drought, or during a hot spell that promises to last more than a week, take these measures while you can still water the lawn when you need to. First, reduce the amount of foot traffic on the grass. Increase the mowing height by 25 percent, and be sure to mow with a sharp blade. Give additional water to areas that dry out fastest, such as high spots or slopes where water drains quickly, and areas near pavement and buildings, which reflect heat. Gradually cut back on watering before drought restrictions are officially imposed.

During extended periods of drought or heat, while water

restrictions are in effect, water only the part of the lawn that you feel is most important, if you are allowed to water at all, and let the rest go dormant. Dormant grass will look brown and dead, but it will usually recover when moisture returns. Avoid all traffic, even walking, on the lawn while it is dormant to prevent any further damage.

When the drought ends, help the lawn recuperate by watering deeply to restart growth. After a week or two, when the lawn is well hydrated and starting to green up, fertilize with a good turf fertilizer. If weeds are a problem, consider using a weed and feed product.

FLOODS AND HURRICANES: Too much water can cause as much damage to a lawn as too little water. Flooding can lead to erosion, deposits of debris, and submersion for varying periods of time, all of which can harm the grass. How to treat your lawn after it's been subjected to flooding depends on how long the lawn was underwater, the amount and type of debris left on the lawn, and the temperature during the flood. Lawns flooded for fewer than four days with less than an inch of silt or debris and a temperature of 60° F or lower have a reasonably good chance of recovery.

To help the turf recover, first remove any debris from the lawn as soon as possible after the water recedes. If there is less than 1 inch of silt on the lawn, use a garden hose to wash off as much of the silt as you can. Then break up the remaining silt crust with a garden rake. Leave the broken crust on

the lawn until the grass is well established again. Apply a good turf fertilizer.

If there is no silt and the lawn has simply been flooded, when the water recedes aerate and fertilize the area. If necessary, reseed to establish a new lawn.

If the lawn was flooded by saltwater, flush with freshwater to leach out the salt.

If the water has eroded the topsoil, renew it by supplementing with 4 to 6 inches of new soil. Alternatively, you can work organic matter (such as peat moss or composted manure mixed with some sand) into the top 4 inches of the subsoil to improve overall soil quality.

Finally, watch out for weeds; there will probably be more weeds than usual after the waters recede. Take measures to eliminate them.

If your lawn has been damaged by drought or flood, consider renting a power aerator, which aerates the lawn faster and more uniformly than hand tools.

All About Weeds

Henbit, a cool-season weed, appears early in spring.

Because annual bluegrass is a grassy weed, applying postemergence herbicides to control it may also harm turf.

Perhaps nowhere else is the classic definition of weeds—plants out of place—more appropriate than in the lawn. Ideally, no plant has a place in the lawn except turfgrass, but keeping the turf totally weed free is impossible. There will always be weeds cropping up, and it's up to you to decide how many you can abide. Weeds are not a monolithic enemy. Some are more tolerable than others. The more you're willing to put up with, the easier your job will be.

Weeds fall into different categories defined by their physical characteristics and growth habits. Weeds are classified as annual, biennial, or perennial. Annual weeds, such as crabgrass, reproduce by seed and live out their entire lives in one year.

Purslane is most troublesome in summer, when turf is stressed by heat and drought.

Removing these weeds before seed forms will go a long way toward controlling the following year's crop.

Biennial weeds, such as mallow, live for two years. Usually the first year's growth is strictly vegetative. The plants don't set seed until the second year. They may reproduce vegetatively or by seed. For best control you must kill or remove the crown and root as well as the seeds.

Perennial weeds live year after year. Many, such as thistle, produce seeds but mainly reproduce vegetatively. With these, each underground rhizome can develop its own roots and become a separate plant, especially after breaking off from the parent plant. To control such weeds, you must kill or remove all stolons, rhizomes, and roots before seeds form.

Both annual and perennial weeds are classified as either cool- or warm-season, depending on the conditions in which they grow best. Cool-season weeds thrive in the mild temperatures of early spring and autumn; warm-season weeds are at their best

Dandelion is a broad-leaved weed with growth characteristics that are much different from those of turfgrasses.

in the heat of summer. They can be especially troublesome in northern lawns, because they grow vigorously at the same time that the cool-season

MOWING AND WEEDS

Though we rarely think of it in these terms, the lawn mower can be a valuable weed control tool if used properly. Studies have shown that high mowing can help to reduce weed populations. One study showed that in a lawn mowed at 2¼ inches, crabgrass cover was reduced from 30 percent to 7 percent in five years. That compares favorably with a plot mowed at 1¼ inches in which crabgrass cover increased from 30 to 33 percent in five years.

High mowing works to retard the growth of many annual weeds. The principle is simple: The taller grass helps to shade and cool the soil and restricts the germination of annual weeds.

If annual weeds do take hold, the lawn mower can help to control their spread. Mowing regularly so seed heads do not develop will prevent weed seeds from becoming established.

grasses are stressed by heat. In the South, they thrive under summer schedules of watering and feeding. When warm-season weeds are a problem in either area, keep watering and fertilizing to a minimum.

Weeds are also classified as broad-leaved or grassy (narrow-leaved). This is an important distinction to remember when using herbicides. Most herbicides labeled to control broad-leaved weeds won't control grassy weeds, and vice versa, so choose the one you need.

Herbicides are either preemergence or postemergence (some are used both ways) and nonselective or selective. Preemergence herbicides kill plants before they emerge from the soil. Postemergence herbicides work after plants start to grow. Nonselective herbicides are toxic to all plant life and are often used to kill an entire lawn before replanting. A selective herbicide will kill one weed but not another, but be cautious. An herbicide labeled to kill grassy weeds could kill the turf too. Always read the labels completely before using the herbicide. Be sure the product is labeled as effective against the weed in question and is safe for the specific grass or cultivar you're growing. And follow the timing guidelines.

There are many ways to control weeds: Pull them, cut them, shade them, mow them, burn them, or kill them with chemicals. Some remedies offer a quick fix; others take time and patience. The rogues' gallery on the following pages gives information for controlling many turf weeds—broad-leaved first, then grassy types.

APPLYING WEED CONTROLS

SPREADING WEED CONTROLS
Drop spreaders are more accurate than broadcast spreaders. They are especially good for spreading products that include both weed controls and fertilizer near flowers and shrubs that you don't want to treat. Use the spreader setting listed on the product label and apply the material in one pass.

SPRAYING WEED CONTROLS
Small sprayers are ideal for spot treatments. The different types of controls require different application techniques. With herbicides, it's important to control the spray to avoid killing the wrong plants. Use low pressure and a nozzle with a fan-shape spray. Spray when the air is still. Otherwise, the pesticide could drift to nontarget plants, which has the potential to harm ornamental plants.

USING HOSE-END SPRAYERS
Hose-end sprayers are particularly useful for treating a large lawn. To ensure even coverage, decide on a pattern with which to cover the lawn, then walk that pattern at a uniform speed, sweeping the nozzle in a constant, smooth motion. Be sure to follow label directions so that you apply the product at the correct rate. You may have to fill the bottle four or more times before you finish.

Broad-Leaved Weeds

Medicago lupulina
meh-dih-CAH-go loop-uh-LEE-nuh

Black medic thrives in dry soils and spotty turf.

BLACK MEDIC

Annual, broad-leaved (sometimes survives as a short-lived perennial).
RANGE: Throughout the United States.
APPEARANCE: With its three-leaflet, cloverlike leaves, this legume is often confused with white clover. Low growing, with trailing, slightly hairy stems, it produces clusters of small bright yellow flowers in late spring to early summer.
GROWTH: Black medic is common in lawns from May through September. It is especially prevalent in dry soils where turf is spotty and in high-phosphorus soils. Though an annual, black medic can be as persistent as a perennial.
CHEMICAL CONTROLS: Eliminate black medic from lawns with Ortho® Weed-B-Gon® Weed Killer for Lawns or Scotts® Turf Builder with Plus 2® Weed Control. Treat from late spring to early summer or in midfall, when the weeds are actively growing.
PHYSICAL CONTROLS: Keep the lawn well-watered to encourage thick turf. Maintain soil phosphorus in the low to medium range, and ensure that the lawn receives adequate nitrogen. Pull or dig the shallow taproots whenever the plants appear.

Plantago major
plahn-TAY-go MAY-jhur

Broadleaf plantain first appears in midspring in thin turf.

BROADLEAF PLANTAIN

Perennial, broad-leaved.
RANGE: Throughout the United States and southern Canada.
APPEARANCE: Egg-shape, wavy-edged gray-green leaves grow in ground-hugging rosettes. Narrow seed heads appear in a long cluster on a central, upright stem.
GROWTH: Rosettes appear midspring in thin and weakened turf. Seed stalks rise early summer through September. The rosette tends to suffocate desirable lawn grasses. Grows from seed and resprouting roots. Seed germinates best in rich, moist, compacted soil.
CHEMICAL CONTROLS: Spray Ortho® Weed-B-Gon® Weed Killer for Lawns in spring or fall when the plants are actively growing; early fall gives the best results by reducing infestation the following year. Repeated applications are often necessary. Or use Scotts® Turf Builder with Plus 2® Weed Control.
PHYSICAL CONTROLS: Proper turf maintenance helps discourage plantain. Collect clippings when mowing. Don't let flower spikes or seeds develop. Aerate the lawn. Dig up and dispose of young plants.

Ranunculus spp.
rah-NUN-kew-luhs

Buttercup flowers appear atop tall, wiry stems; leaves are lower on the stem.

BUTTERCUP

Perennial, broad-leaved.
RANGE: Appears throughout the United States and Canada, but most prevalent in the southeastern, northeastern, and western U.S.
APPEARANCE: The familiar shiny yellow flowers of buttercups appear on several species. Creeping buttercup (*R. repens*) has the largest flowers and deeply cut leaves; bulbous buttercup (*R. bulbosus*) has a bulbous corm at its base. Tall buttercup (*R. acris*) leaves are less lobed. All appear on tall, wiry stems, with flowers high above the leaves.
GROWTH: Though they are usually erect plants, buttercups sometimes stay close to the ground in turfgrass. They die to the ground in winter. Although the bulb may persist, propagation is by seed.
CHEMICAL CONTROLS: Spot-treat with Roundup® Weed & Grass Killer or Ortho® Weed-B-Gon® Weed Killer for Lawns Pull 'n Spray or Ready to Use when the plant is actively growing.
PHYSICAL CONTROLS: Buttercups are easily pulled out by hand.

Achillea millefolium
uh-KILL-ee-uh meel-uh-FO-lee-uhm

COMMON YARROW

Perennial, broad-leaved.
RANGE: Throughout most of the United States, except parts of the Southwest; particularly prevalent in the Northeast and Midwest.
APPEARANCE: This 1- to 3-foot plant has lush fernlike leaves, bright green and up to 2 feet long, and flat white or whitish-yellow flower heads; it forms rosettes in lawns. Leaves are aromatic when crushed. Several other species of yarrow are valued ornamentals.

GROWTH: Yarrow is most common in areas bordering roadways, fields, and vacant lots and thrives in poor, dry soil. It reproduces by creeping underground rhizomes and seeds. The plants persist through the winter.
CHEMICAL CONTROLS: Apply Ortho® Weed-B-Gon® Weed Killer for Lawns or Scotts® Lawn Pro® Step 2 Weed Control plus Lawn Fertilizer anytime plants are actively growing.
PHYSICAL CONTROLS: Dig the plants while still young, before flowers appear and seeds form. Maintaining fertile soil will discourage yarrow.

Common yarrow is easily identified by its ferny foliage.

Rumex crispus
ROO-mecks KRISS-puhss

CURLY DOCK

Perennial, broad-leaved.
RANGE: Throughout the United States.
APPEARANCE: Lance-shape, shiny bright green leaves appear in spring. In summer and fall, the puckered, wavy edges of the leaves are tinted reddish purple. Small greenish flowers appear on a tall, narrow spike that rises from the center of the plant.
GROWTH: Growing from a large brownish taproot, curly dock is a perennial weed that is most active

when grass is suffering from the stress of hot, dry weather, so it benefits from water and fertilizer applied to lawns.
CHEMICAL CONTROLS: Use Ortho® Weed-B-Gon® Weed Killer for Lawns or Scotts® Turf Builder with Plus 2® Weed Control.
PHYSICAL CONTROLS: Pull out curly dock by hand. Any pieces of the root left behind will resprout, so hand digging is seldom successful. Dispose of pulled taproots far from the lawn.

Curly dock arises from a fleshy taproot during hot, dry weather.

Taraxacum officinale
tuh-RAX-uh-kum uh-fish-uh-NAH-lee

DANDELION

Perennial, broad-leaved.
RANGE: Throughout the United States.
APPEARANCE: Everyone recognizes the yellow flowers of dandelions, which appear in early spring, followed by puffy seed heads. Leaves are lance shape.
GROWTH: Dandelions begin growth in early spring and flower as early as April; they continue through summer and fall. The plants reproduce from a long taproot and from seeds.
CHEMICAL CONTROLS: Spray lawns

with Ortho® Weed-B-Gon® Weed Killer for Lawns or apply Scotts® Turf Builder with Plus 2® Weed Control, or spot-treat with Ortho® Weed-B-Gon® Weed Killer for Lawns Ready to Use. Best applied to actively growing plants before seeds ripen.
PHYSICAL CONTROLS: Remove grass clippings to avoid spreading seed. Dandelions thrive in weak, thin turf, so water, mow, and fertilize correctly. Digging dandelions is successful only if you remove at least three-fourths of the root.

Dandelion readily sprouts from both taproots and seeds.

Bellis perennis
BEH-liss purr-EH-niss

Almost too pretty to worry about, English daisy spreads rapidly.

ENGLISH DAISY

Perennial, broad-leaved.
RANGE: Most prevalent in the northern half of the United States.
APPEARANCE: Leaves of this perennial vary from nearly smooth to hairy and form a dense cluster. The daisylike flowers growing on 2-inch stalks have a bright yellow center with white to pinkish outer rays.
GROWTH: English daisy has long since gone from an ornamental to a well-established and fast-growing lawn weed. It grows most rapidly in spring and fall, and in all seasons on the West Coast, if protected from drought and heat. Its presence may indicate low soil fertility.
CHEMICAL CONTROLS: Treat the lawn with Ortho® Weed-B-Gon® Weed Killer for Lawns before July 1. Repeat the treatment around September 15 to control any regrowth. Or use Scotts® Turf Builder with Plus 2® Weed Control.
PHYSICAL CONTROLS: Dig up the fleshy root. Once established, English daisy is difficult to control; remove flowers and seed heads before they drop to avoid spreading their seed. Improve soil fertility.

Convolvulus arvensis
con-VAHL-vew-luss ahr-VEN-siss

Roots of field bindweed may grow to 20 feet deep.

FIELD BINDWEED

Perennial, broad-leaved.
RANGE: Throughout the United States except Florida and Southern California.
APPEARANCE: Field bindweed has long, twining stems that grow across the lawn. Its leaves are arrowhead shaped and up to 2 inches long. Funnel-shape white to pink flowers about 1 inch across appear from spring to fall.
GROWTH: This deep-rooted weed—roots may grow to 20 feet—reproduces by seeds or roots. Roots or pieces left behind from hand pulling will easily resprout. Field bindweed prefers rich, sandy, or gravelly soil but will grow in almost any garden soil. It can injure horses that graze on it.
CHEMICAL CONTROLS: Apply Ortho® Weed-B-Gon® Weed Killer for Lawns from late spring through early summer or from early to late fall. Repeat the treatments as new growth emerges.
PHYSICAL CONTROLS: Keep the lawn well watered to encourage thick turf. Hand pulling or hoeing can't control bindweed; it regrows quickly from the tiniest piece of root left in the soil.

Glechoma hederacea
gleh-KO-mah hed-ur-AY-see-uh

Ground ivy grows via creeping stems that root at the nodes.

GROUND IVY

Perennial, broad-leaved, also known as creeping Charlie.
RANGE: Eastern half of the United States.
APPEARANCE: This member of the mint family sports kidney-shape bright green leaves on hollow stems. Lavender flowers appear from early spring through the summer.
GROWTH: Originally introduced as a ground cover for shady areas, this plant spreads rapidly by creeping stems that root at the nodes. It grows actively from early spring through fall, in sun and shade, as long as the soil is damp. It does particularly well in poorly drained areas. Ground ivy reproduces from seed and its stems root easily upon soil contact.
CHEMICAL CONTROLS: In fall or spring spray lawns with Ortho® Weed-B-Gon® Weed Killer for Lawns or apply Scotts® Turf Builder with Plus 2® Weed Control, or spot-treat with Ortho® Weed-B-Gon® Weed Killer for Lawns Ready to Use.
PHYSICAL CONTROLS: Improve soil drainage; water turf sparingly. Hand pulling is not practical; any piece of stem left in the soil will resprout.

HENBIT

Lamium amplexicaule
LAY-mee-uhm ahm-plecks-ih-KAW-lee

Annual, broad-leaved, also known as dead nettle or bee nettle.
RANGE: Entire United States.
APPEARANCE: Henbit has the typical square-shape main stem of plants in the mint family, of which it is a member. Rounded, toothed leaves grow to ½ inch in diameter. Flowers are trumpet shape and pale purple in color.
GROWTH: Henbit makes its first appearance in late winter or early spring. Its stems lie close to the ground, then curve and grow upright. The stems often root at lower nodes where they touch the soil. Henbit most frequently invades thin areas of lawns having rich soil.
CHEMICAL CONTROLS: Spray lawns with Ortho® Weed-B-Gon® Weed Killer for Lawns or apply Scotts® Turf Builder with Plus 2® Weed Control, or spot-treat with Ortho® Weed-B-Gon® Weed Killer for Lawns Ready to Use. Treat in spring or fall when actively growing.
PHYSICAL CONTROLS: Henbit is shallow rooted and easy to pull.

Henbit is one of the first lawn weeds to appear in spring.

MALLOW

Malva spp.
MAHL-vuh

Annual, sometimes biennial; broad-leaved, also known as cheeseweed.
RANGE: Throughout the United States and Canada; more prevalent in the East.
APPEARANCE: Mallow has hairy stems, 4 to 12 inches long, that spread over the lawn. The stem tips turn upward and have long, round, heart-shape, hairy leaves up to 3 inches wide and slightly lobed. White to lilac flowers, about an inch across, bloom singly or in clusters.
GROWTH: Mallow is most often found in poorly managed lawns and in soils high in manure content. It has a straight, nearly white taproot that is difficult to pull from the soil.
CHEMICAL CONTROLS: Spray lawns with Ortho® Weed-B-Gon® Weed Killer for Lawns or apply Scotts® Lawn Pro® Step 2 Weed Control plus Lawn Fertilizer from midspring to early summer, before young plants have set seed.
PHYSICAL CONTROLS: Maintain a thick, healthy lawn but avoid overfertilizing. If you pull by hand, get as much of the long taproot as possible.

Mallow produces delicate blossoms and a long, tough taproot.

MOUSE-EAR CHICKWEED

Cerastium fontanum vulgare
suh-RAS-tee-um fon-TAH-num vul-GAHR-ray

Annual or perennial, broad-leaved.
RANGE: Throughout the United States and Canada.
APPEARANCE: True to its name, this plant has narrow, fleshy leaves that look fuzzy. Small white flowers appear late spring and early summer.
GROWTH: This weed grows most actively during spring and early summer, when it spreads by means of creeping stems that root at the nodes. Because it grows close to the ground, it withstands low mowing. It grows vigorously in moist, poorly drained, and shaded areas.
CHEMICAL CONTROLS: Spray lawns with Ortho® Weed-B-Gon® Weed Killer for Lawns, or spot-treat with Ortho® Weed-B-Gon® Weed Killer for Lawns Ready to Use. Or use Scotts® Turf Builder with Plus 2® Weed Control. Treat young plants in spring or fall before they go to seed.
PHYSICAL CONTROLS: Hand-pulling is effective only if all parts of the root are removed. Improve drainage and soil fertility. Overseed thinning turfgrasses with improved varieties.

Mouse-ear chickweed is a problem especially in moist, shady areas.

Polygonum aviculare
pah-LIG-oh-num ah-vik-yew-LAH-ree

Prostrate knotweed can be identified by its nonrooting, spreading stems.

PROSTRATE KNOTWEED

Annual, broad-leaved.
RANGE: Throughout the United States.
APPEARANCE: Characterized by tough, wiry stems that radiate from a central taproot, prostrate knotweed forms a mat of foliage with oblong blue-green leaves. Tiny white flowers appear at the junction of leaf and stem.
GROWTH: Propagation is by seed. The spreading stems do not root; however, the plants are deep rooted. Seedlings emerge in late winter to early spring. The young growth often is mistaken for grass. This weed often appears in hard, compacted soils, such as heavily trafficked areas and along sidewalks and driveways.
CHEMICAL CONTROLS: Spray lawns with Ortho® Weed-B-Gon® Weed Killer for Lawns or apply Scotts® Lawn Pro® Step 2 Weed Control plus Lawn Fertilizer from mid- to late spring when the weed is young, with no more than three or four ranks of leaves up its stem.
PHYSICAL CONTROLS: Aerate the turf to correct compacted soil conditions. Maintain a vigorous turf.

Euphorbia supina and *E. maculata*
yew-FOR-bee-uh soo-PIE-nuh
mac-yew-LA-tuh

The spurges can be recognized by their oblong, purple-tinted leaves.

PROSTRATE SPURGE AND SPOTTED SPURGE

Annual, broad-leaved.
RANGE: Eastern two-thirds of the United States and the Pacific Coast.
APPEARANCE: Both of these weeds grow in rosettes, with stems radiating from a central point. Small, oblong leaves have a purple tint. Spotted spurge flowers are pinkish white and inconspicuous.
GROWTH: These annuals form dense mats that can choke out desirable grasses. Plants bloom from spring through summer and set seed in only two weeks. Seed germinates when soil temperatures reach 60° F. Spurge is most often a problem in thin, undernourished turf subjected to drought stress.
CHEMICAL CONTROLS: Apply Scotts® Halts® Crabgrass Preventer in spring before seeds germinate. After plants begin growth, spray lawns with Ortho® Weed-B-Gon® Weed Killer for Lawns or spot-treat with Ortho® Weed-B-Gon® Weed Killer for Lawns Ready to Use.
PHYSICAL CONTROLS: Keep turf irrigated; avoid fertilizing in summer. Can be hand-pulled or hoed.

Tribulus terrestris
try-BEW-luhs tuh-RESS-triss

Puncturevine is a prostrate plant with yellow flowers and stickers.

PUNCTUREVINE

Annual, broad-leaved, also called devil's weed.
RANGE: Throughout the United States except the Far North.
APPEARANCE: This low, branching, creeping plant has 2-inch-long hairy, pale, glossy green leaves divided into five to seven pairs. The hairs can give the plant a silvery appearance. Pale yellow flowers appear from July to September, followed by seed heads with thorny seedpods; these are prickly and are often carried to new locations on clothes, shoes, and pets.
GROWTH: Puncturevine germinates in summer and produces a deep, central taproot. Each plant may spread up to 5 feet across. Puncturevine thrives in infertile, compacted soil in the East and in dry, sandy areas in the West.
CHEMICAL CONTROLS: Apply Scotts® Turf Builder with Plus 2® Weed Control.
PHYSICAL CONTROLS: Aerate the soil to reduce compaction.

Portulaca oleracea
port-yoo-LAH-kah oh-luh-RAY-see-uh

Annual, broad-leaved.
RANGE: Throughout the United States; especially troublesome east of the Mississippi River.
APPEARANCE: Purslane has sprawling, thick, fleshy stems with rubbery leaves. Tiny, five-petaled yellow flowers open when the sun is shining brightly. Cup-shape seedpods produce many small black seeds, which may lie dormant in the soil for years. This plant is seldom found in spring, when the lawn is treated for other weeds.

PURSLANE

GROWTH: It thrives in hot, dry weather, spreading by sprawling stems. It's troublesome in thin areas of the lawn or in new lawns.
CHEMICAL CONTROLS: Spray lawns with Ortho® Weed-B-Gon® Weed Killer for Lawns or spot-treat with Roundup® Weed & Grass Killer. Or apply Scotts® Turf Builder with Plus 2® Weed Control.
PHYSICAL CONTROLS: Maintain dense turf. May also be hand-pulled; remove plants from the garden.

Purslane is a problem in dry, spotty turf and in new lawns.

Potentilla simplex
poh-ten-TIH-luh SIM-plecks

Perennial, broad-leaved.
RANGE: Appears from southern Canada to Alabama, from the Atlantic Coast to the Rockies.
APPEARANCE: Cinquefoils are easily identified by their serrated, five-lobed leaves and bright yellow flowers, which bloom in late spring and early summer. The plants grow close to the ground, have wiry stems, and form tight rosettes. Five-petaled flowers with fuzzy stamens arch over the leaves from spring through summer.
GROWTH: These weeds thrive in nutrient-poor or acid soil. They form

ROUGH CINQUEFOIL

long stolons or short rhizomes with coarse, fibrous roots. Foliage usually dies back in winter.
CHEMICAL CONTROLS: Spray lawns with Ortho® Weed-B-Gon® Weed Killer for Lawns or spot-treat with Roundup® Weed & Grass Killer when the plant is actively growing. Or apply Scotts® Turf Builder with Plus 2® Weed Control.
PHYSICAL CONTROLS: Maintaining good fertility will discourage cinquefoils. Hand-pull or hoe early in the season before flowers appear; by the time flowering begins, the plant has usually formed a long stolon, which is difficult to pull.

Rough cinquefoil has a distinctive, five-part leaf with toothed edges.

Salsola kali var. tenuifolia
sahl-SO-luh KAH-lee
var. ten-yew-uh-FOH-lee-uh

Annual, broad-leaved, also known as tumbleweed.
RANGE: Most of the southern and western United States and Canada.
APPEARANCE: Plants grow 6 inches to 3 feet tall with spreading or erect reddish stems. The leaves on seedlings and young plants are fleshy and cylindrical. As these leaves mature they drop, and narrow leaves ending in spikes appear. From July to October, greenish flowers

RUSSIAN THISTLE

bloom and produce seeds throughout the thistle plant.
GROWTH: Russian thistle prefers areas with dry soil. When the plants mature in early fall, they break off at the soil line and tumble about, distributing the seed.
CHEMICAL CONTROLS: Spray lawns with Ortho® Weed-B-Gon® Weed Killer for Lawns or spot-treat with Roundup® Weed & Grass Killer.
PHYSICAL CONTROLS: Remove seed heads immediately; each plant produces thousands of seeds.

Mature Russian thistle becomes brittle, breaks off, and tumbles about.

Bright orange or salmon flowers identify scarlet pimpernel.

Anagallis arvensis
aahn-uh-GAL-iss ahr-VEN-siss

SCARLET PIMPERNEL

Annual, broad-leaved, also called red chickweed, eyebright, poor man's weatherglass, poison chickweed.
RANGE: Most prevalent in Mid-Atlantic and Pacific states but found throughout the United States.
APPEARANCE: This low-growing, branching plant has small, delicate leaves similar to chickweed, except that it has square stems and, from early summer to early fall, tiny, bell-shape, tubular bright orange or salmon-colored flowers.
GROWTH: Scarlet pimpernel prefers sandy soils. It has a shallow, fibrous root system and will withstand mowing. It reproduces through seeds, which germinate over an extended season.
PHYSICAL CONTROLS: Spray lawns with Ortho® Weed-B-Gon® Weed Killer for Lawns or spot-treat with Roundup® Weed & Grass Killer when the plant is actively growing. Repeat with spot treatment if the plant reappears. Or apply Scotts® Turf Builder with Plus 2® Weed Control.
PHYSICAL CONTROLS: Maintain a thick, healthy lawn and mow at the high end of the scale. Pull out small patches by hand or with a hoe.

Selfheal was valued as a medicinal herb in Colonial times.

Prunella vulgaris
proo-NELL-uh vuhl-GAHR-iss

SELFHEAL

Perennial, broad-leaved, also known as heal-all, carpenter's-weed.
RANGE: Throughout the United States, most common in northeastern United States and southern Canada.
APPEARANCE: Selfheal usually appears as a spreading ground cover that forms dense patches, but it can grow to 15 inches tall in unmown areas. It has oblong leaves that appear on opposite sides of square stems. From June to September it produces spikes of tubular purple and white flowers.
GROWTH: Selfheal prefers shady, moist sites but will grow in sandy, dry areas as well. It propagates by seeds or creeping, rooting stems. Plants are usually evergreen.
CHEMICAL CONTROLS: Spray lawns with Ortho® Weed-B-Gon® Weed Killer for Lawns or spot-treat with Roundup® Weed & Grass Killer when the plant is actively growing.
PHYSICAL CONTROLS: Maintain a thick, healthy lawn and avoid mowing too low. Selfheal can be hoed or hand-pulled if it forms patches. Pull up the whole patch; small pieces that are left will reroot.

Shepherd's purse won't grow in shade and is killed by frost.

Capsella bursa-pastoris
kap-SELL-uh BUHR-suh pass-TOHR-iss

SHEPHERD'S PURSE

Annual, broad-leaved, also called lady's purse, shepherd's bag.
RANGE: Throughout the United States and Canada.
APPEARANCE: This common summer or winter annual has lobed or toothed leaves that form a rosette at the base of the plant and arrow-shape leaves and tiny white flowers on stems 3 to 18 inches tall. Flowers bloom and produce seeds in triangular pods from March until December (or whenever frost hits).
GROWTH: Shepherd's purse tolerates most types of soil but will not grow in shade. Fall frost kills the plants. In warm-winter areas, seeds may germinate in fall, then grow through the winter until the next fall.
CHEMICAL CONTROLS: Spray lawns with Ortho® Weed-B-Gon® Weed Killer for Lawns or spot-treat with Roundup® Weed & Grass Killer when the plant is actively growing. Or apply Scotts® Turf Builder with Plus 2® Weed Control.
PHYSICAL CONTROLS: Shepherd's purse can be hand-pulled or hoed. Small patches can be eradicated by covering with shade cloth.

Veronica officinalis
vuh-RAH-nih-kuh oh-fiss-uh-NAH-liss

Perennial or annual, broad-leaved.
RANGE: Eastern half of the United States except in the extreme South.
APPEARANCE: Several types of speedwell are characterized by small, lobed, and numerous leaves and by tiny white or purple flowers. The scallop-edge leaves are paired and opposite. Heart-shape seedpods form on the stems.
GROWTH: Speedwell is among the earliest of lawn weeds to appear, greening up even in late winter.

SPEEDWELL

Most speedwells are characterized by creeping stems, but some show an erect growth habit. All thrive in cool, moist soils, in thin turf.
CHEMICAL CONTROLS: Spray lawns with Ortho® Weed-B-Gon® Weed Killer for Lawns when plants are flowering or actively growing. Repeated applications may be necessary.
PHYSICAL CONTROLS: Fertilize cool-season lawns in fall instead of in spring. Improve soil drainage.

Speedwell produces white or purple flowers that look like violets.

Trifolium repens
try-FOH-lee-uhm REE-penz

Perennial, broad-leaved.
RANGE: Throughout the United States.
APPEARANCE: Once regularly included in lawn seed mixes, low-growing white clover is characterized by its three-part leaves and white blossoms resembling pom-poms. Though it may be considered attractive, it leaves unsightly brown patches in the lawn when it enters dormancy early in fall and during periods of drought.

WHITE CLOVER

GROWTH: White clover emerges in early spring and spreads by aggressive above- and belowground stems and by seeds. It continues to grow into fall, as long as moisture is adequate. White clover is especially aggressive in high-phosphorus soils.
CHEMICAL CONTROLS: Treat the lawn in spring and early fall with Ortho® Weed-B-Gon® Weed Killer for Lawns, Ortho® Weed-B-Gon® Chickweed, Clover and Oxalis Killer for Lawns, or Scotts® Turf builder with Plus 2® Weed Control. Repeated treatments are often necessary.

White clover grows in early spring and browns out in late summer.

Oxalis stricta
awk-SAW-liss STRICK-tuh

Perennial, broad-leaved.
RANGE: Throughout the United States.
APPEARANCE: Oxalis resembles clover with its three-part, heart-shape leaflets. As flowers mature, cucumber-shape green seedpods take their place. When pods are completely dry, the slightest touch will send their seeds scattering for several feet in all directions.
GROWTH: Yellow wood sorrel grows most vigorously in spring and late

YELLOW WOOD SORREL

summer to fall, especially in moist, fertile soil. This upright perennial sends out roots from its lower nodes.
CHEMICAL CONTROLS: Treat the lawn in spring or late summer to fall, when the weeds are actively growing, with Ortho® Weed-B-Gon® Weed Killer for Lawns or Ortho® Weed-B-Gon® Chickweed, Clover and Oxalis Killer for Lawns. Several treatments are usually needed.
PHYSICAL CONTROLS: Keeping the lawn healthy helps to control oxalis by crowding it out. Plants are relatively easy to pull by hand.

The leaves of yellow wood sorrel look like those of clover.

Grassy Weeds

Poa annua
PO-ah AHN-yew-uh

Annual bluegrass grows vigorously in spring but dies out in summer.

ANNUAL BLUEGRASS

Annual, grassy.
RANGE: Throughout the United States. Considered a winter annual in the South, where it's often used for overseeding.
APPEARANCE: Annual bluegrass has fine green blades and grows in a creeping habit; seed heads, evident at a low height, grow atop the stems, giving a whitish appearance.
GROWTH: Annual bluegrass germinates in early spring or late fall but tends to die out in summer, leaving bare patches in the lawn. Seeds continue to form even under extremely close mowing. This weed is usually found in cool, frequently watered areas, shaded sections of turf, and lawns with compacted soil.
CHEMICAL CONTROLS: Apply Scotts® Halts® Crabgrass Preventer in late summer before seeds germinate. Or for small patches, spot-treat with Ortho® Grass-B-Gon® Grass Killer for Landscapes.
PHYSICAL CONTROLS: Increase mowing height, and remove clippings when seed heads are present. Aerate the lawn to reduce soil compaction.

Echinochloa crus-galli
eh-keen-noh-KLOH-ah krooz-GAH-lee

Deter barnyardgrass by fertilizing your lawn regularly.

BARNYARDGRASS

Annual, grassy.
RANGE: Throughout the United States and Canada.
APPEARANCE: This low-growing grassy weed has reddish or purple stems from 1 to 3 feet long, and smooth ¼- to ½-inch-wide leaves with prominent midribs. The green or purple seed head appears as a coarsely branched panicle.
GROWTH: Barnyardgrass is found in poorly managed lawns with low fertility. It usually appears in summer and fall, reproduces by seeds, and develops into a plant with a shallow root system. Though usually upright, barnyardgrass forms a ground-hugging mat when mowed.
CHEMICAL CONTROLS: In cool-season turf, use a preemergence herbicide such as Scotts® Halts® Crabgrass Preventer. Or for small patches, spot-treat with Ortho® Grass-B-Gon® Grass Killer.
PHYSICAL CONTROLS: Maintain a dense, healthy lawn and fertile soil. The shallow roots can usually be pulled out by hand, or hoed if appearing in patches.

Paspalum dilatatum
pass-PAHL-um dill-uh-TAH-tum

Dallisgrass is a southern perennial that thrives in dry soil.

DALLISGRASS

Perennial, grassy.
RANGE: Coastal states from New Jersey to California and as far north as Missouri.
APPEARANCE: Dallisgrass has coarse blades, somewhat upright in a bunch-type growth. Closely jointed rhizomes appear almost scaly. Stems 2 to 6 inches long emerge from the plant center in a starlike pattern. Seed heads are sparsely branched on long stems. Seeds lie dormant over winter and sprout very early in spring.
GROWTH: This is a summer weed in many areas of the country, but it grows throughout the year in mild climates and thrives in areas that are low and wet.
CHEMICAL CONTROLS: Spot-treat with Ortho® Grass-B-Gon® Grass Killer for Lawns or Ortho® Crabgrass & Nutgrass Killer in spring or early summer. Repeated applications are often necessary.
PHYSICAL CONTROLS: Find methods of draining soil to control dallisgrass in moist areas. Digging up clumps can be difficult because dallisgrass has deep roots.

Eleusine indica
eh-loo-SEEN IN-dih-kuh

Annual, grassy, also called silver crabgrass and yardgrass.
RANGE: Throughout North America, especially warmer climates.
APPEARANCE: Goosegrass looks like crabgrass but is darker green, doesn't root at stem joints, and germinates later in spring. Its smooth, flat stems form rosettes that resemble the spokes of a wheel.
GROWTH: Goosegrass has an extensive root system and grows in lawns that are low in fertility.

GOOSEGRASS

It produces seeds on stalks 2 to 6 inches tall from July to October. The seeds remain dormant over the winter and sprout in spring. The first hard frost in fall kills the plants.
CHEMICAL CONTROLS: Prevent weeds from germinating by applying Scotts® Halts® Crabgrass Preventer in early spring. Spot-treat with Ortho® Weed-B-Gon® Crabgrass Killer for Lawns from midspring to summer.
PHYSICAL CONTROLS: Maintain a thick, healthy lawn of adequate fertility; fertilize regularly.

Goosegrass is easily mistaken for crabgrass but is darker green.

Setaria viridis
seh-TAH-ree-uh VEER-ih-diss

Annual, grassy.
RANGE: Throughout the United States, especially cooler regions, and in parts of Canada.
APPEARANCE: Often called bristlegrass and sometimes mistaken for crabgrass, green foxtail is a semierect bunchgrass. It often has a reddish tint and grows 1 to 2 feet tall. The seed heads are dense and bristly. The seeds sprout from midspring to early summer.
GROWTH: Seeds germinate when the soil temperature reaches 65° F; plants

GREEN FOXTAIL

grow vigorously through the summer. Foxtail dies with the first killing frost. Growth is most vigorous in closely mowed, thin turf that is watered and fertilized frequently in summer.
CHEMICAL CONTROLS: Apply Scotts® Halts® Crabgrass Preventer in early spring, about two weeks before the last expected frost. Spot-treat with Ortho® Weed-B-Gon® Crabgrass Killer for Lawns when plants are actively growing.
PHYSICAL CONTROLS: Remove grass clippings when foxtail seed heads are present; aerate the soil. Plants can also be removed by hand.

Foxtail is a semierect warm-season grass with foxtail-like seed heads.

Muhlenbergia schreiberi
mew-lin-BUR-gee-uh SHRY-bur-eye

Perennial, grassy.
RANGE: Eastern and central United States.
APPEARANCE: With fine blue-green to light green blades and a creeping habit, nimblewill resembles creeping bentgrass. However, its leaves are slow to color in spring, resulting in straw-color patches early in the season in nimblewill-infested lawns. Wiry stems grow up to 10 inches tall—first outward, then upward from the central crown.

NIMBLEWILL

GROWTH: Nimblewill thrives in hot, dry conditions and thin, drought-stressed turf. It greens up in late spring and continues growing until the first killing frost. Stems root at lower nodes as the plants reach out.
CHEMICAL CONTROLS: Spot-treat with Ortho® Grass-B-Gon® Grass Killer for Landscapes or with Roundup® Weed & Grass Killer. Begin control in early spring because seedlings are easier to eliminate than established plants.
PHYSICAL CONTROLS: Dig or pull out plants while still seedlings.

Nimblewill is a creeping grass that goes dormant with the first cold fall weather.

Agropyron repens
ah-gro-PYE-rohn REE-penz

Quackgrass is an invasive creeping grass that browns out in summer.

QUACKGRASS

Perennial, grassy.
RANGE: Throughout the United States except in the extreme South.
APPEARANCE: Quackgrass is characterized by coarse light green to blue-green blades that are rough on their upper surface. In unmowed areas it can grow to 3 feet tall. Roots can reach 5 feet deep or more in a single season. Narrow flower spikes rising from the plant resemble those of rye or wheat. The plant spreads by large white rhizomes.
GROWTH: Quackgrass grows quickly in spring and fall. It is especially vigorous in thin, undernourished turf. Though it sometimes goes unnoticed in early spring, quackgrass becomes quite obvious as it turns brown in summer.
CHEMICAL CONTROLS: Spot-treat with Ortho® Grass-B-Gon® Grass Killer for Landscapes or with Roundup® Weed & Grass Killer.
PHYSICAL CONTROLS: The spread of quackgrass can be checked to some degree by mowing low, cutting the runners, and maintaining dense turf. Hand digging is rarely successful. Patches can be killed by covering them with black plastic sheeting for one year.

Cenchrus spp.
KEN-kruss

Take care when pulling sandbur; its seedpods produce sharp, spiny burs.

SANDBUR

Annual, grassy, also called burgrass and beargrass.
RANGE: Northeastern and midwestern United States, and especially the Southeast and Southwest.
APPEARANCE: This grass grows 6 inches to 2 feet tall and has narrow yellow-green leaf blades ¼ inch wide and 2 to 5 inches long. The blades are attached to flattened stems that may grow upright or spread along the soil.
GROWTH: Plants have shallow, fibrous roots; when growing in mowed lawns, they form low mats. From July to September, seeds are produced inside spiny straw-color burs. Seeds germinate in spring and spread to new areas when burs cling to clothing and animals.
CHEMICAL CONTROLS: Control selectively with Ortho® Weed-B-Gon® Crabgrass Killer for Lawns, or spot-treat with Roundup® Weed & Grass Killer. Prevent sandbur from returning by applying a preemergence herbicide containing trifluralin or Eptam in early spring.
PHYSICAL CONTROLS: Wear gloves to remove plants by hand.

Digitaria spp.
dih-gih-TAH-ree-uh

Crabgrass germinates late and dies with the first frost.

SMOOTH CRABGRASS AND HAIRY CRABGRASS

Annual, grassy.
RANGE: Entire United States.
APPEARANCE: Smooth crabgrass and hairy crabgrass have a prostrate growth habit with coarse light green blades. The blades are short, pointed, and hairy.
GROWTH: This vigorous, warm-season annual grass grows rapidly from early spring until seed heads form in late summer to early fall. It grows especially well in thin turf or in lawns that are watered lightly, underfertilized, or poorly drained. Crabgrass spreads by seed.
CHEMICAL CONTROLS: Prevent crabgrass from sprouting by applying Scotts® Halts® Crabgrass Preventer in early spring, before forsythia blossoms drop. Kill actively growing crabgrass with Ortho® Weed-B-Gon® Crabgrass Killer for Lawns.
PHYSICAL CONTROLS: Crabgrass is not usually a serious problem in lawns with thick, healthy growth. Maintain good management practices: Water deeply and use a high mowing height.

WILD ONION AND WILD GARLIC

Allium spp.
AHL-ee-um

Perennial, grassy.
RANGE: Eastern and central United States.
APPEARANCE: Wild onion and wild garlic are similar in habit; clumps of smooth leaves are topped with small purple or white flowers in early summer. Stems of wild garlic are hollow; stems of wild onion are not. Both plants have a characteristic onion scent.
GROWTH: Often the first plants to green up in the lawn, wild garlic and wild onion grow vigorously from early spring to midsummer, spreading by means of bulbs and roots. Wild garlic may also produce bulblets at its leaf tips; they can fall to the soil and sprout as they mature.
CHEMICAL CONTROLS: Spot-treat with Ortho® Weed-B-Gon® Weed Killer for Lawns when the plants' leaves appear in early spring or whenever plants are actively growing.
PHYSICAL CONTROLS: Mow lawns at low heights in early spring to lessen any infestation; hand-pulling is not practical.

Wild garlic sprouts from small bulbs in early spring.

YELLOW NUTSEDGE

Cyperus esculentus
SYE-pur-uss ess-kew-LEN-tuss

Perennial, grassy.
RANGE: Throughout the United States. A related species, purple nutsedge, is especially prevalent in the Southeast.
APPEARANCE: Though it resembles a grass, yellow nutsedge is actually a sedge. Its coarse light green leaves grow upright from triangular stems. Seed heads appear from July to October.
GROWTH: The plant reproduces mainly from underground tubers but can also reproduce from seeds and underground stems. Tubers store food and are drought tolerant. Yellow nutsedge grows vigorously in summer, especially in moist conditions; it is troublesome primarily in closely mowed lawns.
CHEMICAL CONTROLS: Treat with Ortho® Weed-B-Gon® Crabgrass Killer for Lawns when plants become active in spring. Repeat two or three times 10 to 14 days apart, then again the following spring.
PHYSICAL CONTROLS: Mow high in early summer; water deeply and infrequently. Hand-pulling is not practical.

Yellow nutsedge thrives in moist soil, especially during the summer.

MOSS

Hundreds of species of moss are found in the United States. Though usually not classified as a weed, moss can be a problem in the home lawn.
RANGE: Throughout the United States.
APPEARANCE: Moss is a velvety, low-growing collection of green plants that covers bare soil in shaded areas.
GROWTH: Mosses grow in moist situations, usually in the vicinity of trees. When moss appears, it is usually an indicator that the soil needs fertilizing. Moss usually appears in lawns as a result of poor drainage or poor air circulation, too much shade, or too little fertilizer.
CHEMICAL CONTROLS: Shortly after mowing and when the grass is wet, apply Scotts® Moss Control Granules for Lawns, Ortho® Moss-B-Gon® Granules for Lawns, or Scotts® Turf Builder® with Moss Control.
PHYSICAL CONTROLS: Remove moss with a hand or power rake and reseed with an improved grass variety. Reduce shade and improve air circulation by pruning nearby trees and shrubs; fertilize lawn regularly. Test the soil pH and correct if necessary.

Moss typically grows in moist soil where turf is spotty.

All About Insects

Mole crickets tunnel under turf, feeding on the grass roots.

Insects that suck sap, such as leafhoppers, damage blades.

Hundreds of insect species live in and around your lawn. Chances are you never see most of them. In fact, the great majority of insects do little or no damage to the lawn; only a handful of them cause real harm.

For the best pest control, learn to recognize the bad guys and familiarize yourself with their life cycles and habits. Good control depends on correct identification of the pest as well as a knowledge of its behavior, its biology, and the conditions that favor it.

Some pests thrive where it is warm and dry; others prefer cool or moist conditions. Other important factors that determine which types of pests you might encounter in your lawn include degree of shade or sunlight, amount of slope, and soil type.

If you suspect you have a lawn pest problem, examine your lawn thoroughly to find the culprit. Pests are often found first in stressed areas— at the edge of the lawn or in shady or wet areas. They are not usually distributed evenly throughout the lawn. Look for spots that have discolored, stunted, or distorted grass. Now take a closer look. Get down on your hands and knees and concentrate your attention on the area of the damage. Insects tend to proceed outward from a central point; therefore, they

PEST-RESISTANT GRASSES

During the past several years, waging war against turf insects has become easier due to the introduction of pest-resistant grasses. These are varieties of perennial ryegrass and fescue that carry microscopic fungi known as endophytes. Endophytes repel a broad range of insects, including greenbug, armyworm, billbug, cutworm, and sod webworm. Take advantage of the latest breeding advances and look for seed blends that indicate on the package that they offer insect resistance.

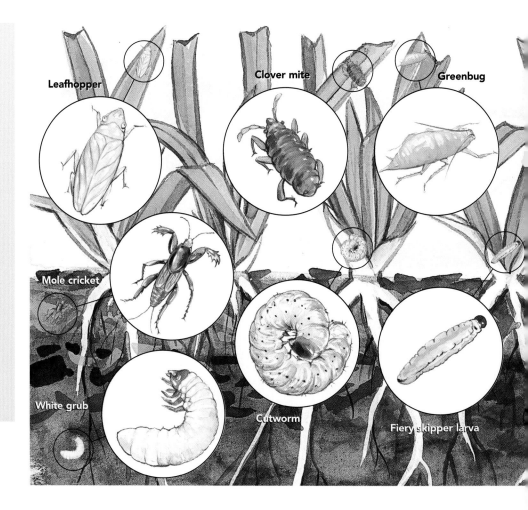

Leafhopper

Clover mite

Greenbug

Mole cricket

White grub

Cutworm

Fiery skipper larva

are generally most active on the outside edge.

Part the leaves of grass and look into the thatch layer. Focus on a specific area for several seconds and watch for insect movement. Look for evidence of pest infestation, such as the pellet-shape green droppings left by sod webworms.

If leafhopper, scale, or spider mites are at work, you can find them by examining the stems, leaves, and crowns of the plants. Chinch bugs live here too, as well as in the thatch layer.

Other insects, such as sod webworms, can be driven to the surface of the soil by drenching a patch of lawn with pyrethrum, a natural pesticide. Mix 1 tablespoon of a pyrethrum pesticide (1 to 2 percent) in 1 gallon of water. Mark off about 1 square yard and apply the entire gallon mixture as evenly as possible using a sprinkling can. If those insects are present, within a few minutes they will rise to the surface of the lawn, where you can then spot and identify them.

Grubs are controlled by products designed to prevent them. If your lawn has been prone to grub damage in the past, apply a season-long grub control such as Scotts® GrubEx®.

If you find insect pests, eradicate them according to the recommendations in the bug gallery found on the following pages.

Sod webworms feed on plants just above the thatch layer, leaving spots of dead, thin turf.

INSECTS

FEEDING ON BLADES:
Billbug adult
Chinch bug
Clover mite
Greenbug
Leafhopper

FEEDING ON CROWNS:
Cutworm (lawn moth larvae)
Fiery skipper (lawn moth larvae)
Sod webworm (lawn moth larvae)
Armyworm (lawn moth larvae)
Billbug larvae

FEEDING ON ROOTS:
Ground pearl
Mole cricket
White grub
Wireworm

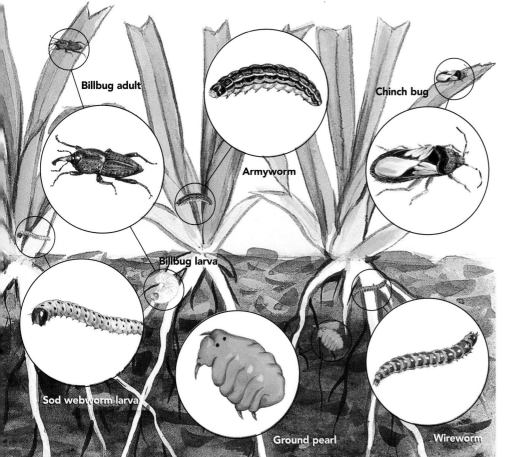
Billbug adult
Armyworm
Chinch bug
Billbug larva
Sod webworm larva
Ground pearl
Wireworm

Turf pests live in and damage all areas of grass, from the blade tips to the crown to the roots. For example, greenbugs feed on the blades. Billbugs live in the thatch. Grubs spend their lives underground feeding on the roots.

Armyworms are southern pests, especially on Bermudagrass lawns.

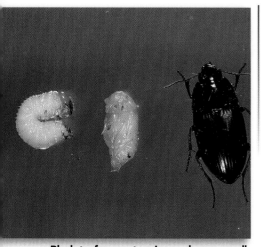

Adult billbugs lay eggs in the stems of grass plants.

Black turfgrass ataenius grubs are small larvae that consume grass roots.

ARMYWORMS

SYMPTOMS: Small patches of brown turf have grass blades eaten off to the soil surface in circular patches. Tiny, fuzz-covered eggs are on the grass. **INSECT APPEARANCE:** Armyworm caterpillars are light tan to dark brown with yellow, orange, or dark brown stripes down the lengths of their backs. They are ¾ inch to 2 inches long. Adult moths are tan or mottled gray with a wingspan of about 1 inch. They fly only at night or on overcast days. In daylight they hide in the soil around grass roots.

LIFE CYCLE: Moths appear in late spring to early summer and lay hundreds of eggs at a time on the grass. Larvae hatch from eggs within 10 days and begin feeding. You may see the larvae hanging from threads on the grass. In the South, there may be as many as six generations a year. **CONTROLS:** Apply Ortho® Bug-B-Gon® MAX™ Insect Killer for Lawns or Scotts® Turf Builder® with SummerGuard®.

BILLBUGS

SYMPTOMS: A small and distinct circular pattern becomes yellowish or brown when billbugs are feeding on the lawn. Because the larvae feed on roots, grass plants within the dead areas easily lift out of the soil. A sawdustlike white debris can be found on the ground around the affected plants. **INSECT APPEARANCE:** Billbug larvae—which do most of the damage—are legless white grubs about ⅜ to ½ inch long. Brownish gray adults have long snouts, which they use for burrowing and chewing off plants.

LIFE CYCLE: Overwintering adults emerge in midspring, when they often can be found crawling on sidewalks and driveways. Soon after, they lay eggs on grass stems. Grubs emerge in May or June, then tunnel into the stems. From there, they eventually migrate into the lawn's root zone. **CONTROL:** Apply Ortho® Bug-B-Gon® MAX™ Insect Killer for Lawns or Scotts® Turf Builder® with SummerGuard®. Water and fertilize the lawn to stimulate new growth. Reseed or resod large areas. Maintain proper soil moisture and fertility.

BLACK TURFGRASS ATAENIUS

SYMPTOMS: Larvae damage appears similar to that inflicted by white grubs and Japanese beetles. Small patches of turf begin to turn brown in late spring or early fall as the larvae hatch and feed. Afterward, the dead patches of lawn are easily rolled back. **INSECT APPEARANCE:** Adults are ¼-inch-long shiny black beetles. Larvae are small grubs, less than one-fourth the size of other grubs, and white with a brown head.

LIFE CYCLE: Adults overwinter in the soil and emerge in spring, when you'll see them flying during the hottest part of the day. They lay eggs in late spring; the larvae emerge soon afterward and begin feeding. There may be a second generation produced during late summer. **CONTROL:** Control with Scotts® GrubEx® Season-Long Grub Control as soon as damage is apparent. To prevent damage next year, apply GrubEx in late April.

CHINCH BUGS

SYMPTOMS: Large, distinct, circular yellowing patches appear brown in the center and generally occur only in sunny areas of the lawn.

INSECT APPEARANCE: Adult chinch bugs are from 1/16 to 1/4 inch long. Most are black with white wings, each of which has a distinctive triangular black mark. Young chinch bugs are wingless and red with a white back stripe.

LIFE CYCLE: Adults overwinter in both the North and South, emerging as early as March. They feed by sucking the juice from grass blades, injecting a poison that causes blades to turn brown and die. They are most active during hot, dry weather.

CONTROL: Apply Ortho® Bug-B-Gon® MAX™ Lawn & Garden Insect Killer spray or Ortho® Bug-B-Gon® MAX™ Insect Killer for Lawns granules as soon as you see damage. Or use Scotts® Turf Builder® with SummerGuard®. Prevent recurring damage by treating every two months until frost.

Chinch bugs can be recognized by their objectionable odor.

CRANE FLIES

SYMPTOMS: Beginning along the edges of the lawn, patches of turf brown out and die. Heavily infested areas show a brownish paste covering the soil where the grass has died.

INSECT APPEARANCE: The grubs (which do the damage) are brownish gray with a tough, leathery texture. (Grubs are also called leatherjackets.) They are about an inch long and are usually found on top of and just below the soil surface. Adult crane flies resemble long-legged mosquitos, except they are much larger and do not bite.

LIFE CYCLE: Adults lay eggs in lawns in late summer; overwintering larvae emerge. The grubs begin feeding on grass roots in early spring and continue to feed through the summer.

CONTROL: Use Ortho® Bug-B-Gon® MAX™ Insect Killer for Lawns with Grub Control. Treatment is most effective in early April.

Adult crane flies produce root-eating larvae.

CUTWORMS

SYMPTOMS: Cutworms leave 1- to 2-inch-wide patches of brown grass in new and established lawns; the plants are eaten off at soil level.

INSECT APPEARANCE: The larvae of cutworms are plump and smooth and almost always curl up when disturbed. They are most often gray, brown, or black; some are spotted or striped. They often grow to 2 inches long. The adult moths are dark and fly at night.

LIFE CYCLE: Moths lay their eggs in late summer. After hatching, larvae overwinter in trash and clumps of grass and resume feeding early in spring (only at night). They mature into moths in July or August.

CONTROL: Apply Ortho® Bug-B-Gon® MAX™ Insect Killer for Lawns or Scotts® Turf Builder® with SummerGuard®.

Cutworms sometimes feed on grass blades.

FIRE ANTS

SYMPTOMS: Large mounds of soil, 1 to 2 feet in diameter and more than 1 foot high, appear throughout the lawn.

INSECT APPEARANCE: Ants are reddish in color and up to ¼ inch long. The head is normal size, but the last segment of the antenna is longer than that of other ants.

LIFE CYCLE: Fire ants are most often a problem in sunny sites and clay soils in southern states.

CONTROL: Use Ortho® Orthene® Fire Ant Killer, drenching the mound itself along with the area around the mound to a distance of 4 feet. Or broadcast Ortho® MAX™ Fire Ant Killer Broadcast Granules. Or use Scotts® Turf Builder® with Fire Ant Killer.

Fire ants (right) ruin lawns with their massive mounds (above).

GRASSHOPPERS

Grasshoppers are turf pests only in severe drought.

SYMPTOMS: Grasshoppers chew grass plants down to the crown.

INSECT APPEARANCE: Various species range from brown to yellow to green in color and vary in length from 1 to 2 inches. They are all characterized by a long body, large hind legs for jumping, and prominent jaws. Young grasshoppers lack fully developed wings.

LIFE CYCLE: Females lay eggs from midsummer into fall. Eggs hatch from late winter to late summer, depending on the climate. After nymphs molt they begin feeding; if food supplies grow scarce, they move across the countryside devouring greenery. Grasshoppers are generally not a problem on the lawn unless swarms of them move in. This may happen in rural areas during drought, when normal food sources are scarce.

CONTROL: Treat large infestations with Ortho® Systemic Insect Killer applied with a sprayer or use Scotts® Turf Builder® with SummerGuard®. For moderate long-term control, use a bran bait with *Nosema locustae*, a grasshopper disease organism. If the number of grasshoppers is small, handpick them early in the morning, when they move more slowly.

GREENBUGS

Greenbugs may feed on grass blades in summer.

SYMPTOMS: Rust-color patches of grass appear under trees when greenbugs are feeding. These patches of grass turn brown and die as the insects continue to feed. The damage then spreads to sunny parts of the lawn. Grass blades may have yellow or rust-color spots with a dark center. Underwatered or overfertilized Kentucky bluegrass lawns are particularly susceptible to this insect.

INSECT APPEARANCE: A type of aphid, greenbugs are small, light green, and wedge shape.

LIFE CYCLE: Greenbugs begin feeding in late spring and continue throughout the summer, producing many generations. They suck sap from—and inject a poison into—grass blades as they feed. Greenbugs rarely build up to populations large enough to do damage. But if you sweep your hand over the grass and see greenbugs scatter, there are enough to require action.

CONTROL: Use Ortho® Systemic Insect Killer applied with a sprayer over the entire lawn.

LEAFHOPPERS

SYMPTOMS: Areas of the lawn look pale or even white, and small white spots appear on individual blades of grass as leafhoppers suck the sap from them. Like aphids, they produce a sticky substance called honeydew. Affected grass also has a stunted, thinned appearance.

INSECT APPEARANCE: Tiny (less than ⅛ inch long even when fully grown) leafhoppers are wedge shape and pale green, yellow, or gray. They fly or hop from blade to blade. Immature leafhoppers resemble the adults but are paler and do not have wings.

LIFE CYCLE: Adults overwinter in debris and emerge in midspring. Females lay eggs in early summer; within two weeks nymphs emerge. Leafhoppers are nearly always present in lawns, but no action is needed unless there is a severe infestation. If you kick up a swarm of leafhoppers with each step, it's time to take action.

CONTROL: Use Ortho® Systemic Insect Killer or Ortho® Bug-B-Gon® MAX™ Insect Killer Ready-Spray®.

Leafhoppers are tiny insects that suck sap from grass blades.

MITES

SYMPTOMS: Patches of pale yellow, straw-color, or silvery grass, and thin, browned-out turf.

INSECT APPEARANCE: Microscopic mites are virtually impossible to spot without magnification. Mites have eight legs and are insect related rather than true insects. Clover mites are ⅟₃₀ inch long and green to red in color; Bermudagrass mites are even smaller. Mites feed on the underside of grass blades. You may see their fine webbing on the plants.

LIFE CYCLE: Mites are most active during hot, dry weather; they may overwinter in thatch or other protected areas. Though they may be present on the lawn, mites rarely reach numbers high enough to cause problems. Mites do the most damage in times of water stress.

CONTROL: Use Ortho® Bug-B-Gon® MAX™ Insect Killer Ready-Spray®. Adequate watering helps to keep down spider mite populations.

Mites can be recognized by the presence of webs on grass blades.

MOLE CRICKETS

SYMPTOMS: Mole crickets cause irregular streaks of brown and wilted grass that pulls up easily. You can find the crickets' tunnels with your fingers or sometimes even see them if the ground is bare. The lawn feels spongy underfoot.

INSECT APPEARANCE: Mole crickets are about 1½ to 2 inches long and brown or grayish brown. They look similar to the common cricket, except their head is large and they have notable short, fat front legs.

LIFE CYCLE: Mole crickets are a problem primarily in the Atlantic and Gulf Coast states. Adult crickets eat grass roots, and their nighttime tunneling—6 to 8 inches below the soil surface—damages roots and causes the soil to dry out beneath the lawn. Adult crickets emerge from the soil in spring to mate.

CONTROL: Treat with Ortho® Bug-B-Gon® MAX™ Insect Killer spray in June or July. Mow and water thoroughly before applying. Or treat the lawn with Ortho® Bug-B-Gon® MAX™ Insect Killer for Lawns granules.

Mole crickets do most of their damage by burrowing under turf.

Nematodes are microscopic worms that feed on grass roots.

NEMATODES

SYMPTOMS: Signs of nematode trouble are often subtle. They include slow-growing grass that is thin and yellowish and susceptible to summer drought. If you examine the grass roots, they may appear stubby and shallow, possibly showing galls.

INSECT APPEARANCE: These pests are invisible to the naked eye. Identifying them requires laboratory analysis by a professional.

LIFE CYCLE: Among the most plentiful life forms on earth, nematodes exist primarily in moist soil and soil debris. They travel slowly through the soil and attach themselves to plant roots. They suck juice from the plants and inject a chemical that causes galls to form.

CONTROL: Treatment is determined by nematode type, soil type, and climate; professional analysis is needed. Keep grass as healthy as possible. Hiring a professional to fumigate the soil before planting a new lawn is recommended, especially in the South, where nematodes are more prevalent. Soils high in organic matter resist nematode infestation.

Rhodesgrass scale attacks St. Augustinegrass near its crown.

SCALE INSECTS

SYMPTOMS: In late summer, the grass turns brown and dies in irregular patches.

INSECT APPEARANCE: These tiny (1/16 to 1/8 inch long), legless insects are covered with a hard white shell. Bermudagrass scale can be found clinging to stems; scale insects known as ground pearls (which are pinkish in color) attach themselves to roots. They look like bumps on leaves and roots.

LIFE CYCLE: These insects feed on the stems and roots of Bermudagrass, St. Augustinegrass, and centipedegrass, mostly in the South and Southwest. In warm climates, they can be active for as long as the grass is growing. They are especially prevalent in sandy soils. If scale-caused brown patches spread throughout the lawn, or if grass stems are covered by scales, treatment may be required.

CONTROL: No pesticides are labeled for control of scale insects in lawns, although the insects might be controlled by insecticides applied for other pests. The best defense is to keep your lawn growing vigorously.

Sod webworm adults (above) lay eggs in turf, where they feed.

SOD WEBWORMS

SYMPTOMS: Dead patches are 1 to 2 inches wide, with grass blades chewed off just above the thatch line. Usually prevalent in the hottest, driest areas of the lawn.

INSECT APPEARANCE: Sod webworm larvae are slender, black-spotted grayish caterpillars approximately 3/4 inch long and sluggish in their activity. They hide during the day in shelters constructed of bits of grass and debris. The buff-color moths, which fly in zigzag patterns over the lawn at dusk, have two snoutlike projections on their head.

LIFE CYCLE: Overwintering larvae emerge and feed at night or on overcast days in spring. They mature into moths in early summer and lay eggs, which hatch into larvae and repeat the cycle. There may be as many as three generations per season.

CONTROL: Apply Ortho® Bug-B-Gon® Multi-Purpose Insect Killer Ready-Spray® or Ortho® Lawn Insect Killer Granules when you notice large numbers of moths. Use Scotts® Turf Builder® with SummerGuard®.

WHITE GRUBS

SYMPTOMS: Irregular shape dead brown patches of turf, particularly in late spring or early fall, roll back easily like a section of carpet. Birds, moles, raccoons, and skunks may damage a lawn looking for grubs.
INSECT APPEARANCE: White grubs have curled C-shape bodies from ¼ to ¾ inch long. They are creamy white with a yellow or brown head and dark hind parts. Adults vary in appearance, because white grubs are the larvae of Japanese beetles, June bugs, rose chafers, Asiatic beetles, and others.
LIFE CYCLE: Grubs overwinter and begin feeding early in spring. Adult beetles appear in late spring or early summer. A second generation emerges in late summer and feeds in autumn. Cut and lift a 1-square-foot section of sod. If you see more than six white grubs in the soil, it's time to apply a treatment.
CONTROL: Apply Scotts® GrubEx® Season-Long Grub Control from spring through summer. Water well after applying.

White grubs feed primarily on the roots of cool-season grasses.

WIREWORMS

SYMPTOMS: Wireworm damage to the lawn resembles grub damage: Irregular patches of turf turn brown and die. Dead sod is easily lifted from the soil.
INSECT APPEARANCE: Wireworms, which are the larvae of click beetles, are hard-shelled brown worms that grow to about 1½ inches in length. The adult beetles are ½ to ¾ inch long with flattened dark brown bodies, often with darker markings.
LIFE CYCLE: Wireworms overwinter as adult beetles or pupae. In spring, beetles lay eggs in sod; larvae emerge soon after and begin feeding on plant roots. These insects, which remain as feeding larvae for two to six years, are most often found in moist soils.
CONTROL: To check for wireworms, bury whole potatoes about 3 inches deep in various locations around the lawn. If, after three or four days, the potatoes are crawling with wireworms, it's time to take action. (Be sure to destroy the potatoes; do not compost.) There are no chemical controls labeled for wireworms. In areas of serious infestations, numbers can be reduced by burying potatoes every 3 feet and removing and destroying them after four days.

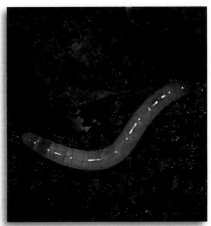

Wireworms are the hard-shelled larvae of click beetles.

MOLES AND GOPHERS

Moles and gophers are rodents that live underground. Moles feed on earthworms, grubs, and other insects; gophers eat plant roots or entire plants. Each causes damage to the lawn by severing grass roots, raising sod, and in the case of gophers, eating sections of the lawn.

Moles are 6 to 8 inches long with velvety gray to black fur. Gophers are brown with small eyes and ears and conspicuous pouches on either side of their mouth. When moles are present you will notice raised ridges, 3 to 5 inches wide, that crisscross the lawn. These ridges sometimes turn brown because tunnels have destroyed the grass roots. Gophers create crescent-shape mounds of soil on the lawn. On close probing, you will find a hole underneath each mound. Gophers usually are found in the western United States.

Trapping or baiting is the best way to eliminate gophers from your yard. Moles are harder to control with traps or poisons because of the temporary nature of their tunnels.

Moles damage lawns as they search for insects on which to feed.

All About Diseases

Top-dress lawns to retard disease development.

Turf diseases may appear as circular or irregular shape patches of dead or brown grass (top) or as spots on individual blades of grass (above).

Virtually all turf diseases are caused by soil-dwelling fungi. Often these pathogens are held in check by beneficial fungi and other microorganisms. It is only when conditions become favorable for the pathogens that they gain the upper hand. How do conditions change to favor pathogens? Generally through improper care.

Fungal diseases are easier to prevent than to cure. Although you can control turf diseases with fungicides, your first action should be to understand the conditions that give rise to disease, then correct them so diseases won't get started in the first place.

Planting the right grass seed blends for your climate will help minimize the chance of disease. A grass that is poorly adapted to an area is weaker and more susceptible to attack.

Apply fertilizer in the right amount at the right times for your lawn. Use controlled-release fertilizers, since fast-growing turfgrass is lush and succulent and thus easy prey

for disease organisms. With some grasses, too much fertilizer may also encourage thatch, which not only harbors disease-causing organisms but weakens the grass by slowing the passage of water and nutrients. Thatch should be no thicker than ½ inch.

Watering in the morning rather than at night can retard fungal growth by allowing the lawn to dry out during the day. Some diseases thrive on wet roots; others multiply rapidly on moist leaves. Avoid frequent, shallow watering. Irrigate only when necessary, and then water deeply and thoroughly.

Correct soil compaction, which weakens grass plants by restricting root growth. Aerate the soil, then top-dress with topsoil or compost.

Controlling lawn diseases

The control of lawn diseases should begin with an accurate diagnosis of the problem.

A thick thatch layer can lead to diseased turf.

This diagnosis is often based on knowledge of the types of problems to which your particular grass is susceptible. Once you have eliminated insects and cultural problems as causes of the symptoms you see, consider disease as the source.

Lawn diseases vary in severity from year to year and from place to place, depending on weather conditions, lawn-care practices, and the disease organisms themselves. Some diseases are active in certain seasons; others can strike at any time.

Fungicides

In general, fungal diseases are more difficult to control with chemicals than are insects, simply because of the way in which fungi grow in the infected plants. They are able to penetrate the plant and proliferate there, which makes them hard to reach.

Many fungicides are available for use on home lawns. They are categorized as either contact or systemic. Contact fungicides work on the outside of plants. They are best applied before the disease appears. For example, if you know from experience that a particular disease attacks your lawn at a certain time of year, prevent the disease by applying the appropriate fungicide two weeks beforehand.

Systemic fungicides work from inside plants and are usually the most effective. However, some systemic fungicides are specific and control only certain diseases.

In heavy shade, replace grass with a shade-loving ground cover.

Both systemic and contact fungicides are sold in several forms: as granules you spread over the lawn, as powders you mix with water and spray, and as liquids you dilute and spray. Granules tend to be the easiest to apply uniformly.

If accidentally ingested, most fungicides are much less toxic to animals than are insecticides. However, many fungicides irritate the skin. Handle them with care. Always follow the product label to the letter, especially when it comes to application rates and timing.

The following pages list the most common diseases of turfgrass, including symptoms of the diseases and suggested controls. Some chemical controls are preventive only and won't help once the disease strikes. Other fungicides can be used to control an already established disease.

Before buying a fungicide, read the label directions to ensure that the product can be used to control the disease in question on the grass species in your lawn.

Use a screwdriver to check soil compaction and dryness.

DISEASE DETECTIVE

Diagnosing a particular disease is a challenge because many diseases have similar symptoms. Moreover, as a disease develops over time, these symptoms may change. Here are some general clues that can help you. For best results, look closely at individual plants and at the lawn as a whole.

Plant Symptoms	Cause
FUNGAL GROWTH ON THE BLADE	
Long black streaks of powdery spores	Stripe smut
Powdery white dust	Powdery mildew
Red or orange powder	Rust
Gray fungus that is easily rubbed off	Slime mold
SPOTS ON LEAVES BUT NO FUNGUS VISIBLE	
Reddish brown to blue-black circles or ovals	Leaf spot
Straw-color bands with a reddish brown border	Dollar spot

Lawn Symptoms	Cause
CIRCULAR DISEASED AREA	
Present in late winter or early spring	Snow mold
Present in summer, spring, or fall (1 inch to 4 feet or more in diameter)	
Mushrooms present	Fairy ring
No mushrooms	Brown patch
Present in summer, spring, or fall (1 to 8 inches in diameter)	
Throughout the lawn	Dollar spot
Only in full sun, showing green center	Fusarium blight
In low areas and often in streaks	Pythium blight
IRREGULAR SHAPE DISEASED AREA	
New lawn seedlings wilt and die	Damping-off
Mature lawn affected; spots on leaves	Leaf spot

Brown patch forms large brown to gray spots with wet-looking edges.

BROWN PATCH

SEASON: Mid- to late summer.

APPEARANCE: Large, irregular circular areas, up to several feet in diameter, appear throughout the lawn. The patches usually have a brownish to gray discoloration, with a water-soaked appearance around the edges of leaves and stems.

FAVORABLE CONDITIONS: High temperatures (75° to 95° F), heavy or dense thatch, high humidity, lush or weak growth from overfertilizing, and excessive moisture create perfect conditions for this disease to thrive.

SUSCEPTIBLE GRASSES: This is a serious disease in the South on centipedegrass and St. Augustinegrass. It also attacks bentgrass, Bermudagrass, ryegrass, fescue, and zoysiagrass.

CULTURAL CONTROL: Avoid excessive fertilization with fast-acting fertilizers, reduce shade and thatch, and water deeply but infrequently only in the morning. Keep the lawn on the dry side.

CHEMICAL CONTROL: Apply Ortho® Lawn Disease Control or Scotts® Lawn Fungus Control, spraying or spreading when disease is first noticed and at least three more times at 14-day intervals.

Dollar spot develops numerous small brown patches across a lawn.

DOLLAR SPOT

SEASON: Spring to fall.

APPEARANCE: Grass dies off in small spots from 1 to 5 inches in diameter, but the spots may coalesce into large areas. Spots are usually bleached from tan to straw color. Cobwebby white fungus threads may be seen in early morning.

FAVORABLE CONDITIONS: Moderate temperatures, excess moisture, and heavy thatch all contribute to this disease; it is common near foggy coasts. Nitrogen-deficient lawns develop more dollar spot.

SUSCEPTIBLE GRASSES: It is most severe in bentgrass and Bermudagrass but also attacks Kentucky bluegrass, fescue, and ryegrass.

CULTURAL CONTROL: Feed lawn to promote healthy growth. Keep grass as dry as possible; water deeply when necessary but refrain from watering at night.

CHEMICAL CONTROL: Apply Ortho® Lawn Disease Control or Scotts® Lawn Fungus Control when the disease is first evident, then every 28 days until symptoms are gone.

Fairy ring appears as a circle of dark green grass around a lighter patch.

FAIRY RING

SEASON: Spring to fall.

APPEARANCE: This fungus appears as rings of dark green grass surrounding areas of dead or light-color grass. The rings can be produced by the growth of any one of more than 50 kinds of fungus. Grass inside the ring dies because water cannot penetrate the cobwebby surface of the fungus, which lies near the top of the soil. After prolonged wet weather, mushrooms (the fruiting bodies of the fungus) may appear around the edge of the ring, where the fungus is actually growing.

FAVORABLE CONDITIONS: Fairy rings usually develop in soils that contain undecomposed, woody organic matter, such as dead tree roots or old construction materials.

SUSCEPTIBLE GRASSES: All.

CULTURAL CONTROL: Fairy ring is not a turfgrass disease and does not cause long-term harm to the lawn. Its effect can be masked by applying fertilizer outside the ring and not within. Aerate the ring to improve water penetration.

CHEMICAL CONTROL: None recommended.

FUSARIUM PATCH (PINK SNOW MOLD)

SEASON: Fall to spring.
APPEARANCE: Circular patches are 1 to 8 inches in diameter; tiny white or pink masses are sometimes seen on dead leaves. Fungal threads, also white or pink, become visible in early morning. Blades of grass are light tan and stick together. Small, gel-like white or pinkish spore masses are occasionally seen on dead leaves. This disease is called pink snow mold if it develops under snow or at the margins of melting snowbanks.

FAVORABLE CONDITIONS: Cool temperatures (40° to 60° F) and moisture.
SUSCEPTIBLE GRASSES: Ryegrass, fescue, zoysiagrass, colonial and creeping bentgrasses.
CULTURAL CONTROL: Reduce shade, improve soil aeration and drainage, and avoid excessive nitrogen fertilization in fall.
CHEMICAL CONTROL: Apply Ortho® Lawn Disease Control according to directions.

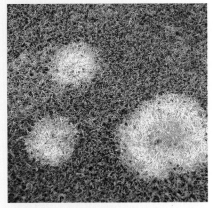

Fusarium patch appears in spring or fall as circles of dead grass.

LEAF SPOT

SEASON: Spring to fall.
APPEARANCE: The most obvious symptom of this disease is elongated circular spots on the grass blades. These spots have a brown or straw-color center with black to purplish borders.
FAVORABLE CONDITIONS: Cool (50° to 70° F), moist conditions are most favorable for the growth of leaf spot. The spots first appear on grass in shady areas, most commonly during wet, humid weather or in lawns that are sprinkled lightly and frequently or mowed too closely.

SUSCEPTIBLE GRASSES: Kentucky bluegrass, fescue, and Bermudagrass.
CULTURAL CONTROL: Reduce shade, improve aeration and drainage, and mow at correct height. Water early in the day to keep grass dry at night.
CHEMICAL CONTROL: Spray lawn with Ortho® Lawn Disease Control or Scotts® Lawn Fungus Control when leaf spotting is first noticed. Make at least three more applications 7 to 10 days apart.

Leaf spot shows up as small brown circles on grass blades.

NECROTIC RING SPOT

SEASON: Spring to fall.
APPEARANCE: "Frog-eye" patterns occur in the lawn; these are small circles of dead grass with a tuft of green grass surrounding and enclosing them. Infected leaves turn reddish purple.
FAVORABLE CONDITIONS: This fungus is most active at relatively low temperatures (58° to 82° F), but dead spots may not become apparent to the naked eye until warm, dry periods in the middle of the summer, when they seem to suddenly appear.

SUSCEPTIBLE GRASSES: The most susceptible is Kentucky bluegrass, particularly 'Arboretum', 'Fylking', 'Park', and 'Pennstar'. Bentgrass, creeping bentgrass, and fine fescues can also be attacked.
CULTURAL CONTROL: Dethatch and aerate. Follow correct mowing and watering practices. Cut grass as high as possible to keep the soil cool. Fertilizing well helps grass recover.
CHEMICAL CONTROL: Apply Scotts® Lawn Fungus Control.

Necrotic ring spot makes itself known with circular frog-eyes.

One symptom of powdery mildew is a dusty coating on grass blades.

POWDERY MILDEW

SEASON: Early summer to fall.
APPEARANCE: First symptoms are light patches of dusty white to light gray growth on grass blades, especially during cool, rainy weather. Lowest leaves may become completely covered. Although generally not too serious a problem, it can become severe if not controlled. Heavily afflicted areas look as though they've been covered with lime or flour or sprayed with a coat of white paint.
FAVORABLE CONDITIONS: Slow or nonexistent air circulation, shade, and high humidity with temperatures of 60° to 70° F.
SUSCEPTIBLE GRASSES: Kentucky bluegrass, zoysiagrass, and Bermudagrass. Lawns growing rapidly because of excessive use of nitrogen fertilizer are extremely susceptible.
CULTURAL CONTROL: Reduce shade and improve air circulation; avoid overwatering and overfertilizing.
CHEMICAL CONTROL: Treat lawns with Ortho® Lawn Disease Control when the mildew is first seen.

Pythium blight appears as patches of soft and slimy grass.

PYTHIUM BLIGHT

SEASON: Summer.
APPEARANCE: The first indication of this disease is the occurrence of irregular patches a few inches in diameter. In those areas, the grass blades appear water soaked, soft, and slimy. The blades soon wither and fade to light brown or straw color, sometimes reddish brown, particularly if the weather is sunny and windy. Then the patches join to form large damaged areas that often reach several feet in diameter. In the early morning, a cottony white fungus can usually be seen on the blades of the diseased plants.
FAVORABLE CONDITIONS: High temperatures and excess moisture.
SUSCEPTIBLE GRASSES: Tall fescue, bentgrass, Bermudagrass, Kentucky bluegrass, annual ryegrass.
CULTURAL CONTROL: Avoid overwatering. Make sure the lawn has good drainage. Do not sow seed more thickly than recommended. Water lawns in the morning; avoid mowing wet grass in hot weather.
CHEMICAL CONTROL: None recommended.

Red thread shows up as red or pink strands of fungus on grass blades.

RED THREAD

SEASON: Fall.
APPEARANCE: Small spots that appear water soaked enlarge rapidly to cover a large part of the leaf. As the spots dry, the leaves fade to a light brown or tan. Pink webs bind the grass blades together. Later, the fungus forms thin, fingerlike red to pink structures at the tips of grass leaves, which gives the lawn a reddish cast.
FAVORABLE CONDITIONS: It is most damaging in spring and fall in temperatures of 68° to 75° F and high humidity. Low levels of nitrogen favor its development. When grass growth slows down due to a lack of nitrogen, the disease becomes more prevalent.
SUSCEPTIBLE GRASSES: Red fescue, ryegrass, bluegrass, and bentgrass.
CULTURAL CONTROL: Keep soil pH at 6.5 to 7.0 and increase nitrogen level; water deeply in the morning.
CHEMICAL CONTROL: Spray severely affected lawns with Scotts® Lawn Fungus Control.

RUST

SEASON: Midsummer to fall.
APPEARANCE: The lawn takes on a rust-color cast, especially noticeable from a distance. Dustlike spores, the main symptom of this disease, form in circular or elongated groups on grass blades. Anything moving through a severely infested area will be covered by the spores and may spread the disease.
FAVORABLE CONDITIONS: Moderately warm, moist weather. Dew that lasts for 10 to 12 hours promotes germination. Stress that restricts growth favors rust.

SUSCEPTIBLE GRASSES: It can affect most types of turfgrass, but Kentucky bluegrass is damaged most frequently.
CULTURAL CONTROL: Keep the lawn growing rapidly by applying a high-nitrogen fertilizer and by watering properly. Mow every four or five days and remove clippings.
CHEMICAL CONTROL: Treat severely affected lawns with Ortho® Lawn Disease Control.

Rust occurs as reddish pustules or dust on the surface of grass blades.

STRIPE SMUT

SEASON: Spring to fall.
APPEARANCE: Infected grass plants are usually pale green and stunted. Stripes or streaks made up of spore masses form along the surface of the grass blades, turning from light to dark. Leaves that are affected by stripe smut curl, die, and become shredded by the advancing disease. Affected plants can occur singly or in spots ranging in size from a few inches to more than a foot in diameter. These affected areas will usually grow somewhat more slowly and are generally shorter than surrounding healthy grass.

FAVORABLE CONDITIONS: The moderate temperatures of spring and fall encourage stripe smut. Hot, dry weather often alleviates it.
SUSCEPTIBLE GRASSES: Some varieties of Kentucky bluegrass as well as bentgrass.
CULTURAL CONTROL: Keep thatch to a minimum, reduce fertilizer applications, and avoid overwatering.
CHEMICAL CONTROL: Treat with a systemic fungicide in October or early March.

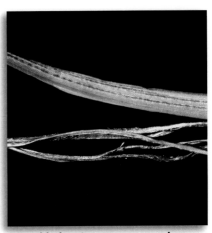

Dusty-black stripe smut stunts plants, which turn pale green.

SUMMER PATCH

SEASON: Midsummer.
APPEARANCE: It begins as scattered light green patches up to 8 inches in diameter that turn dull tan to reddish brown. In larger diseased patches, the easiest symptom to recognize is the "frog-eye" pattern—an apparently healthy green patch of grass that is partially or completely surrounded by a ring of dead grass.
FAVORABLE CONDITIONS: Hot, dry, and windy weather creates an excellent climate for summer patch. It's most prevalent when hot (89° to 95° F), sunny days follow warm

periods that have alternated between wet and dry weather.
SUSCEPTIBLE GRASSES: Bentgrass, turf-type tall fescue, perennial ryegrass, and some bluegrasses.
CULTURAL CONTROL: Dethatch and aerate regularly; apply nitrogen lightly and often. Light, frequent watering helps keep summer patch under control during drought.
CHEMICAL CONTROL: Apply Ortho® Lawn Disease Control or Scotts® Lawn Fungus Control.

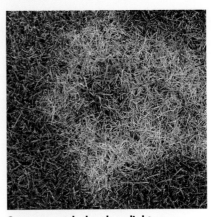

Summer patch develops light green areas up to 8 inches wide.

Resources

ORTHO

Ortho provides a comprehensive support system for its customers. The company's specialists can be reached through its helpline (800-736-0191), by mail (Ortho Consumer Service, P.O. Box 190, Marysville, OH 43040), or on its website (www.Ortho.com). The website includes a wealth of information and access to special services. Among the features you'll find:

■ **BASICS** This section is designed to give you a general understanding of the most fundamental topics in gardening. Whether you are planning a formal garden or simply a pot of geraniums, the site shows you the best way to care for all your plants—from watering to pruning.

■ **PROJECTS** Easy step-by-step directions, product recommendations, and expert advice will help you achieve beautiful results.

■ **FAQS** Browse categories or search for the answer you need from a list of common questions.

■ **PLANNERS AND TOOLS** This section of the site includes insect and weed finders, an annual program builder, and a chart to help you identify your grass.

■ **DISCUSSION FORUM** Join other gardeners to share tips, problems, and inspiration.

THE SCOTTS COMPANY

The Scotts Company provides extensive support for its customers. You can find help from lawn-care specialists by calling the company's toll-free number, 800-543-TURF (8873), or by e-mail through its website, www.Scotts.com. You'll find numerous other tips and services on the website, such as:

■ **LAWN & GARDEN CARE PLANNER** Create a customized month-by-month maintenance plan.

■ **GROW MAGAZINE** This online source provides in-depth articles on lawn and garden topics.

■ **LAWN CARE OR GARDENING REMINDER SERVICE** Register and you'll be contacted by e-mail so you know just what to do—and when—to maintain a healthy lawn and garden.

■ **VIDEO QUICK TIPS** Watch lawn and garden videos right on your computer.

NATIONAL SOURCES

■ **NATIONAL TURFGRASS EVALUATION PROGRAM** Provides results of national testing of all major turfgrass species. This program is partially funded by the U.S. Department of Agriculture.

REGIONAL SOURCES

■ **COOPERATIVE STATE RESEARCH, EDUCATION, AND EXTENSION SERVICES (CREES)** Located in most counties of the United States, these agencies offer local information and publications from experts who know your area and climate. To find your local extension agents, look in the blue government pages in your telephone directory; they are usually located under local government, agriculture. Or check this website: www.csrees.usda.gov/

■ **UNIVERSITY PROGRAMS** Often connected to county extension agencies, turfgrass, horticulture, and agriculture departments at universities provide cutting-edge research on grasses, troubleshooting, and maintenance. Here are a few of them; search for others by typing "lawns" and your region into an Internet search engine:

Cornell University
www.hort.cornell.edu

Guelph Turfgrass Institute
www.uoguelph.ca/GTI

Kansas State University
www.oznet.ksu.edu/dp_hfrr/turf/welcome.htm

Michigan State University
www.turf.msu.edu

Penn State University
www.worldcampus.psu.edu/pub/turf/ele

Purdue University
www.agry.purdue.edu/turf

Rutgers University
turf.rutgers.edu

Texas A & M University
aggieturf.tamu.edu

University of California, Davis
www.ipm.ucdavis.edu

University of California, Riverside
ucrturf.ucr.edu

University of Connecticut
www.canr.uconn.edu/plsci/agr-ts.htm

University of Florida
turf.ufl.edu

University of Illinois
www.turf.uiuc.edu

University of Maine
www.ume.maine.edu/~nfa/lhc/hortic.htm

University of Missouri
agebb.missouri.edu/turf

Washington State University
turf.wsu.edu/index.html

Index

METRIC CONVERSIONS

U.S. Units to Metric Equivalents			Metric Units to U.S. Equivalents		
To Convert From	**Multiply By**	**To Get**	**To Convert From**	**Multiply By**	**To Get**
Inches	25.4	Millimeters	Millimeters	0.0394	Inches
Inches	2.54	Centimeters	Centimeters	0.3937	Inches
Feet	30.48	Centimeters	Centimeters	0.0328	Feet
Feet	0.3048	Meters	Meters	3.2808	Feet
Yards	0.9144	Meters	Meters	1.0936	Yards
Square inches	6.4516	Square centimeters	Square centimeters	0.1550	Square inches
Square feet	0.0929	Square meters	Square meters	10.764	Square feet
Square yards	0.8361	Square meters	Square meters	1.1960	Square yards
Acres	0.4047	Hectares	Hectares	2.4711	Acres
Cubic inches	16.387	Cubic centimeters	Cubic centimeters	0.0610	Cubic inches
Cubic feet	0.0283	Cubic meters	Cubic meters	35.315	Cubic feet
Cubic feet	28.316	Liters	Liters	0.0353	Cubic feet
Cubic yards	0.7646	Cubic meters	Cubic meters	1.308	Cubic yards
Cubic yards	764.55	Liters	Liters	0.0013	Cubic yards

To convert from degrees Fahrenheit (F) to degrees Celsius (C), first subtract 32, then multiply by ⁵⁄₉.

To convert from degrees Celsius to degrees Fahrenheit, multiply by ⁹⁄₅, then add 32.